A GENTLEMAN ON WALL STREET

A GENTLEMAN ON WALL STREET

*My life
in flying, skiing,
finance,
love
and more.*

HARRY A. JACOBS JR.

with

NICK TAYLOR

Outskirts Press, Inc.
Denver, Colorado

Outskirts Press, Inc.
http://www.outskirtspress.com

ISBN PB: 978-1-4327-5206-4
ISBN HB: 978-1-4327-5343-6

Outskirts Press and the "OP" logo are trademarks belonging to Outskirts Press, Inc.

PRINTED IN THE UNITED STATES OF AMERICA

This book is for my beloved wife of almost forty-nine years, Marie, and my beloved wife of almost ten years, Joannie; for my daughter Nancy and her children Patricia and Nicolle; and for my son Terry, his wife Sally, and their sons Steven and Andrew.

Table of Contents

Introduction ix

Childhood, Family, Early Life 1

Lincoln School 5

The Depression 7

Dartmouth 9

Flying: Discovering a Passion 13

Marie 17

The War Years 21

Flight Instructor 25

Young Parents with No Place To Go 29

My Unhappiest Time 31

Bache: Warming To Wall Street 33

A Growing Family 37

Climbing the Ladder 39

Golden Times: Zürs and Beyond With Nancy and Terry 41

Wall Street Social Life 47

The Start of My Political Conversion 49

Family Time 53

Bache: Scramble at the Top 57

Turmoil on Wall Street.. 61
My Political Conversion Is Complete 65
New Houses 69
Bache: Going Public... 71
Bache: Fighting for the Top Spot 73
New CEO 77
Challenges 103
Crisis: The Belzbergs 107
Crisis No. 2: The Hunts and Their Silver 111
The Belzberg Fight Escalates....................................... 115
Pru-Bache.. 119
Culture Clash 123
Outside Interests 127
John and Annie Glenn... 131
Marie 135
My Brothers and Sisters.. 141
Joannie 145
The Next Generations... 153
Lessons.. 157
Changes on Wall Street 163
My Investment Philosophy 169
Remarkable Women 173
Friends and Meaningful Others 175
Some Thoughts at the End of the Day 183

Introduction

I've had an interesting life. I don't know if the pundits would agree. Charlie Rose hasn't been calling and I haven't heard from Larry King in quite a while. Book publishers aren't writing big checks with my name on them. But a lot of folks would think my story is worth reading.

The pundits and publishers aren't knocking on my door because my experiences go back. They forget that the past informs the present and the future. I'm eighty-eight years old as I write this. I served in the Army Air Forces during World War II and have been flying ever since. I had a long and happy marriage to my first wife and a short and happy marriage to my second. I have wonderful children, stepchildren, grandchildren, great grandchildren, and friends. I rose to the heights of Wall Street, met a lot of rich and famous people, and still took time to get to know my family. Speaking of Wall Street, I even remember when gentlemen worked there.

This memoir is first of all for my family and my friends. I want to let the people I love know how I feel about them, and I don't want my stories to get lost in the haze of generations as my father's and my brother's did. I guess that means I have an ego. But in case anybody else **is** interested, I also want to make some comments on my life and times.

I was on Wall Street for almost forty years, and I've seen the damage greed can do – and has done – to depositors, investors, taxpayers, and public confidence in the financial system. Excessive leverage combined with lack of regulation over the creation of exotic (rhymes with toxic) investment vehicles was a train wreck waiting to happen, and it did. I'm not saying things were better in the past, but the Great Depression of the 1930s, which I lived through, provides some lessons about prudence that we need to learn again.

I hope we can do that. I also hope we can regain a tone of respect in our political dialogue. I hope that we can erase, or at least lessen, our divisions and come together somewhere around the middle so that our great country can be as great for future generations as it has been for me and mine.

Most of all, I hope that you enjoy what you're about to read.

Childhood, Family, Early Life

I was born on June 28, 1921. We lived in a seventeen-room brownstone house at 117 West 85th Street in New York City. It was my father Harry Allan Jacobs' work of art, where he took the clients of his prominent architectural practice to get business. The dining and living rooms were two stories high, with sculptures and paneling his friends had designed. He had lived in Paris for six years and learned architecture at the Ecole des Beaux Arts. He designed the Hotel Elysee on East 54th Street, the "Monastery" on West 48th Street occupied by the Friars Club for forty years, and residences for prominent New Yorkers. His work won him the Prix de Rome and he was a fellow of the American Academy in Rome and belonged to several other arts and architectural societies and served on city boards.

He was fifty years old when I was born, which makes me think I was an accident, or at least an afterthought. My closest sibling was my sister Jane, nine years older; then my sister Katherine, whom everyone called Kitty, fourteen years older; then my brother Robert, who was sixteen years older. I was truly the baby of the family, and Bob was more like my father than my brother because of the age difference.

Although I was named for him, I didn't know my father very well. He was sick a lot throughout my childhood, and I was just eleven when he died of complications after a gall bladder operation in August, 1932. He was only sixty. My mother, who was Elsie Wolf before they married, was at least ten years younger, and she was much closer and more vivid in my memory. Bob used to call her "the Saint." He meant no irony at all. She was all good and he just loved her, and so did I.

She and my father were part of a group called "Our Crowd." Stephen Birmingham published a book by that name in 1967. Its subtitle was "The Great Jewish Families of New York." They were German Jews from the middle and upper middle class who came to America in the 1840s and became a part of the business and social structure of New York. They formed the root structure of such firms as Lehman Brothers, Goldman Sachs, Kuhn Loeb, and others. My father was the architect to those people, and so I always thought we were poor. And we were, compared to them, but we weren't really poor.

We weren't really Jewish, either, at least as far as I could tell. My parents always said they were Jewish, but they weren't in the religious sense. They didn't belong to or attend a synagogue, and they observed Christian holidays like Christmas and Easter, or at least the meals and family gatherings connected to those holidays. That confused me, and still does. And my mother belonged to the Ethical Culture Society, which uncomplicates religion by teaching that you should do good on this earth and at the end you go to sleep. None of that altered the fact that "Our Crowd" were an amazing group of people, and it's a legacy of which I'm very proud.

My childhood was totally happy. We had four "in-help" at the West 85th Street house – the cook, the chambermaid, the laundress, and my nurse, Nora Mae Phelan, who was with our family for forty-five years. She was wonderful, very Irish, and I was very close to her. We spent summers at Lake Placid, at a rambling old house on Buck Island my family bought in 1923. Those summers in the beautiful Adirondacks were an endless dream of swimming, boating, tennis, and making friends with the local kids who lived there all year round.

Lincoln School

I started in school at Dalton, the exclusive prep school on the Upper East Side. But in the fifth grade I switched to the Lincoln School, a progressive school for gifted children that was run by the Columbia University Teachers' College. It was on West 123rd Street near the Columbia campus and was endowed by John D. Rockefeller Jr. It's closed now, and that's a shame. I loved that school. The faculty members were magnificent. Josephine Mayer, the social studies teacher, was a lifelong influence. It was she who taught me how to clarify my thoughts by outlining, and to this day, when I have to give a speech or make a presentation, I start my preparations with an outline. Gordon Merrick taught math, and his class was also memorable.

As we got into the higher grades, the world had no limit. We would start a class in the fall and just go as fast as we could, not following any pre-set lesson plan but just learning as much as we could. Approaching the ninth grade, I was entered at Deerfield Academy, a boarding prep school in Massachusetts. It was – and is – a fine school, but I refused to go. Lincoln was just so challenging! We worked like hell! There were a lot of people smarter than me in that school, but I graduated first in my class academically and by then I had the equivalent of at least a year of college.

When I was in the seventh grade I became aware that a lot of my classmates at Lincoln lived in the area around Columbia in the section of Manhattan called Morningside Heights and their families belonged to Riverside Church in the same neighborhood. Riverside is another institution that John D. Rockefeller Jr. helped get off the ground. It is an interdenominational Protestant church with a history of progressive thought and social action. I started going there intensely. For a kid that meant Friday night bowling, Saturday morning basketball, Sunday morning Sunday school and church, and Sunday afternoon literary club. That all became too much by the time I reached tenth grade at Lincoln because the school was too demanding. But by then, I knew I wanted to go to church for the rest of my life.

The Depression

In 1938 my mother put the house on West 85th Street up for sale. She said the neighborhood had gone down but I think the Depression, then in its eighth year, had taken its toll of her finances. It was about this same time that the sleek 1927 Chris Craft we used to ferry us between the mainland and Buck Island at Lake Placid disappeared. In its place appeared a fifteen-foot wooden boat powered – if that's the right word – by a seven and a half horsepower Johnson outboard. The help at Lake Placid had dwindled to two, and when a buyer offered $10,000 for the West 85th Street house my mother took it and moved to a two- bedroom apartment at 1065 Lexington Avenue on the East Side. It had a maid's room, and she took just one of the in-help with her. Again, I thought we were poor.

And again, being poor was relative. I remembered the crews of Works Progress Administration laborers I saw working on roads around Lake Placid and building a new town post office. Some of them might once have owned resorts like ours until they went bust in the 1929 Wall Street crash that triggered the Depression. As I putt-putted around the lake, it seemed as if every fourth house I saw was boarded up and rotting away, their owners bankrupted. Back home, my grandmother Wolf had fallen on her version of hard times. Her husband had been one of the founders of the Standard Toch Chemical Company, so they were comfortable. When I was young I remembered her being chauffeured around by a driver named Stanley in a luxurious Pierce Arrow. It had separate compartments for the passengers and driver, who normally endured the elements but could snap a plastic top over his head when it rained. By the end of my high school years she still employed Stanley as her chauffeur, but he was driving a Ford.

Dartmouth

I entered Dartmouth College in the fall of 1938 along with three of my Lincoln School classmates. Hanover, New Hampshire, had a familiar feel. It was only about four hours by car, across the south end of Lake Champlain at Port Henry and through the Green Mountains, from Lake Placid, and it was a continuation of a countryside I loved. Dartmouth was a great school for anyone who loved to ski, as I did. I had learned to ski at Lake Placid the year before I went to Dartmouth, and loved it right away. Now some of the best skiing in the East was only a short drive away at places like Stowe and Woodstock, in Vermont, and I looked forward to winter weekends.

Dartmouth had a fine ski team, and while I wasn't good enough to be competitive I was enthusiastic enough to land as the team manager after a couple of years. I met great friends that way, including Mo Distin from Saranac Lake near Lake Placid. He was the greatest four-event skier I ever saw at Dartmouth; we remained close throughout our lives. I met Bill Scheefer at the Middlebury Carnival, one of the regular intercollegiate ski meets hosted by area colleges. Bill skied for St.

Lawrence. It turned out that he lived at Saranac Lake, too, and today he is my best friend.

In keeping with Ivy League tradition, Dartmouth was no slouch in academics either, but I didn't find it as challenging as Lincoln School. I was disappointed that the courses weren't open-ended. In one of my freshman classes the professor gave us a syllabus showing what we would do in September and what we'd be doing in January. I thought, How could that be? At Lincoln we went as far and as fast as we could even if it meant working Saturdays. So that was a shock. You learned what the lesson plans said you were supposed to learn and that was it.

Nevertheless, some fine professors taught there. My personal favorite was Ramon Guthrie. He was one of the American Lafayette Escadrille pilots who flew for France during World War I, for which he won the Silver Star, and stayed on in France where he earned a doctorate at the University of Toulouse and got married. He was an acclaimed poet who had also written novels. Most of all, for me, he was a great, great teacher like you read about in books. He taught my minor subject, nineteenth century French literature, and was an authority on Marcel Proust.

Professor Guthrie made Proust's writing come alive for me. It is hard to describe exactly what I found in *Remembrance of Things Past* that so affected me. Proust seemed to have X-ray vision in his view of life, like looking at the outside of a building and seeing through to its core, all the bricks and beams and posts and joists and the stairways leading from one level to another, and how they all interlocked to form a whole.

What was more, Proust most felt the anguish of one who had been jilted in love, and I had just been jilted in love. Katie Sprackling was the culprit's name. She was also dating my longtime friend Billy Lowenthal from Lincoln School days and also Jerry Tallmer, who was editor of *The Daily Dartmouth*. I thought I had the upper hand because she would develop headaches when she dated them and then she and I would meet for late dates around ten-thirty. The day I got her "Dear John" letter breaking it off between us, I went to see Jerry to discuss it and I found him in his dorm room holding the same letter. She jilted all three of us for an Air Corps navigator named Jack Schwartz, whom she eventually married.

When I told Professor Guthrie of my heartbreak, he gave me the best possible answer. "I envy you your anguish," he said. It was such comments that opened Proust to me, and I took every other course he ever gave. He was one of the primary influences on my early life and I loved him dearly. He was also courageous. Much later, during the Vietnam War, he returned his Silver Star to President Johnson to protest the United States' Vietnam War policies. Because of Ramon Guthrie, even today I keep a copy of Proust by my bedside and dip into it from time to time for insight (and maybe a little nostalgia).

My brother Bob had gone on to emulate my father and become an architect after college at Amherst and architecture school at Columbia. He was already, by then, becoming famous in his own right in the field with his firm, Kahn and Jacobs. But I approached my college education with no thought of following the family profession. I majored in political science and minored, as I said, in nineteenth century French literature. I had no firm political convictions in those days; I was much more interested in recreation. What politics I had tended Republican, a result of Our Crowd conservatism with regard to money. I had started taking French at Lincoln School and continued at Dartmouth, learning enough to read Proust in his native language and to even speak a little, but my specialties pointed me in no particular career direction.

Flying: Discovering a Passion

Up to my junior year, my college experience had been indifferent. A sinus infection during my freshman year had set me back. My grades had suffered, partly from feeling that I wasn't challenged. I got three Bs and two Cs after leading my class at Lincoln School. The fraternities all passed me over the next year, and that ticked me off. I was a junior when Katie Sprackling dumped me, but by then I was getting three As and two Bs, so things were improving.

That year also brought me the first glimmering of a career goal, something I thought I could pursue with commitment and passion. Around 1938, the administration of Franklin Delano Roosevelt, then in its second term, started a government-sponsored program to train pilots. It was called the Civilian Pilot Training Program but FDR assumed those pilots would end up in the military if America had to go to war. Germany and Italy were both spoiling for a fight, and were training pilots by the droves. The Thayer School at Dartmouth, the college's engineering school, offered the program for two years starting in 1940, by which time Europe was at war and it seemed more and more likely the U.S. would get involved.

I had an idea I'd like flying all along. I was twelve or fourteen when I sent an application to the U.S. Army Air Corps at Randolph Field in San Antonio, Texas. In those between-wars years, the military branches were probably grateful for every application they received, but even then they drew the line at kids who were barely in their teens. So when the Civilian Pilot Training Program came to Dartmouth, I jumped in.

The program started with ground training that fall and moved quickly into flight training. There were twenty of us in the group. We flew out of the Bugbee Flying Service at a little dirt field outside White River Junction, Vermont. The planes were Piper Cubs with 65-horsepower engines. They didn't go very fast, but the first time up I knew I loved it.

The instructor's name was Earl Blanchard, and he had a way of getting your attention. The cabin configuration placed the instructor's seat in front and the student's directly behind, with control sticks in front of each seat that were linked to each other. When we made mistakes Earl would bang his stick back and forth and the one in back would bang between your knees and leave you black and blue. All that stick rattling didn't affect the Piper's handling very much. They were sluggish but forgiving and just fishtailed a little bit.

The notorious Vermont winter didn't slow us down. When it snowed we took off and landed on skis. I worked hard all that fall and received my private pilot's license on December 2, 1940, compliments of Uncle Sam. If anybody in my family worried about the dangers connected with flying, they never let me know about it.

The following summer the civilian training program added a secondary program for acrobatics. I signed up for the course. We flew out of Roosevelt Field on Long Island in the old WACO – the initials stood for Weaver Aircraft Company of Ohio – UPF-7s. These were biplanes that were widely used in training. Ideally they were powerful and fun to fly. But I should have had the guts to quit because the equipment was a mess. The planes were all falling apart. The control for the stabilizer, the leading edge of the horizontal tailpiece that steadies the plane in flight, was a knotted cord by your hand.

I was coming in one day and I don't think I made a bad landing but the left landing gear collapsed. I went up on my nose and over on my back and landed on my head. Gasoline was dripping all over the engine, but I was knocked out so I didn't turn the switches off. Fortunately a friend of mine, Jimmy Israel, was in the next building and he ran over and pulled me out by my feet. I was coming to but I didn't know I was upside down so when I opened my safety belt I fell down on my head again. I've had near-misses since, but that was my first and only crackup, knock wood. Jimmy, sadly, died near the end of World War II in the Pacific, when his loaded B-24 exploded on takeoff.

Marie

The Japanese attacked Pearl Harbor on the morning of December 7, 1941. Until then talk of war at Dartmouth had focused on Europe and how England was bravely holding off the Germans with the help of American Lend-Lease. Some isolationists still argued that the U.S. should stay out of the conflict, but even Ernest Martin Hopkins, the conservative Republican who was Dartmouth's president, was for intervening and most of the students agreed with him. Pearl Harbor ended the debate. It brought America into World War II, and millions of lives were changed as a result.

I was out rabbit hunting at Lake Placid and didn't hear about it until seven o'clock that night. It's impossible to convey the shock and astonishment I felt. I got back to Dartmouth around ten that night and found the whole campus talking. The next day, some students packed their bags and left school to enlist. As a senior with just a few months to go, I decided to finish school but to volunteer in the meantime, to go in after I graduated.

It sounds strange to say, but the event that changed my life even more than Pearl Harbor occurred a little over a month later, on the second Saturday in January, 1942.

Bud Silverstein and I had made the half-hour run from Dartmouth to Woodstock to ski at Gilbert's Hill. The run was justly famous as the site of the first rope ski tow in the country. I think I read somewhere that it was powered by a Model T Ford engine. On the other side of the hill was Suicide Six, the small resort owned by Lawrence Rockefeller. Bud had followed me as the Dartmouth ski team manager. But on this day I found something on the slopes I liked better than the skiing. There going down the hill was a beautiful blonde girl. I said, "I'm going to marry her."

I caught up to her at the bottom of the hill and introduced myself. Her name was Marie Stevens, she had grown up on a farm in Etna, outside Hanover, and she worked at Wells, Hudson and Granger, a local architect that was making ends meet designing Work Projects Administration projects for the government. She was obviously popular, but I persuaded her to go on some ski dates. At first Bud tagged along. We called ourselves "Ski Three" after a movie that was out at the time, but three soon became a crowd.

In March, Dartmouth was skiing against McGill University at Mt. Tremblant outside of Montreal. I asked Marie to go but she couldn't. When I got back one of my roommates told me Marie had gone skiing with Bud. I was blind with rage. Even when I learned he'd taken a fall and broke his ankle, I thought it served him right. "No more 'Ski Three'", I told Marie. And she agreed.

We started seeing each other all the time. I lived off-campus and she had moved from Etna to an apartment in Hanover when she took a new job in the Dartmouth bursar's office. We lived only two or three blocks apart, so that made it easier. I skipped night astronomy classes to spend time with her. We went skiing every weekend. When spring came, we saddled the farm's horses and took long rides in the evening.

What an amazing time it was! With my pilot's license, I knew the war was waiting for me when I graduated. But for the moment there was no future, only the present.

Easter came early that year, on April 5. She invited me to have Easter dinner with her family. It was the first time I had met them. When I got there her father went into the yard and caught and killed a chicken and that was the centerpiece of a real farm meal – chicken and gravy. It was a great meal and a lovely occasion; her parents were so kind and altogether nice. But as time went on I noticed that Marie got increasingly jumpy. I didn't know why until I got up and asked where the bathroom was and she, somewhat embarrassed, pointed me to a privy out back.

It was true that Marie and I came from vastly different economic and religious situations. I thought my family was poor by comparison with the Our Crowd banking moguls, but Marie's family really was. The farm just scraped by. Her father worked part time for the Post Office, delivering mail along a rural route, to help make ends meet. Her very religious family attended a small Baptist Church in Etna that was part of their lives, while I thought I wanted to become a Catholic. I was taking instruction until the priest at Dartmouth, Father Sliney, who played golf with Marie, told me she was thoroughly Protestant and a "mixed marriage" might not work. That ended my flirtation with Catholicism.

None of that really mattered to either one of us, and not to my family or to hers. I was madly in love and so was she. Her parents thought that whatever Marie wanted she should have, and if I was what their daughter wanted well then, that was good for them. And that same month, April of 1942, when I brought Marie down to New York to meet my mother and my brother and sisters, she became the heroine of the family overnight. Everybody adored her.

The first week in May we went up to my family's place at Lake Placid. The house's caretaker, Charlie Martin, acted as our chaperone on my mother's orders, since she didn't think Marie should be there without somebody to keep an eye on things. I proposed that weekend, and was overjoyed when she said yes.

The War Years

Our future was certain and uncertain at the same time. In April, I had enlisted as a Flying Cadet in the U.S. Army Air Forces, its name changed from the Air Corps the year before. The war was sure to require every pilot Uncle Sam could lay his hands on, and I was ready to serve. In the meantime, I didn't want to spend a minute without Marie. Dartmouth's Class of 1942 graduated in May, and once my diploma was in hand I was thrown back on the time-honored military dictum, "Hurry up and wait."

The waiting took all summer. I spent the time in Lake Placid. Marie was in Hanover. Gas rationing was on, but each of us could get enough so that we could meet halfway. She drove to Port Henry, New York every weekend that summer. I would meet her there and we would drive back to Lake Placid, where my mother was now in residence as chaperone. I'd drive her back to Port Henry on Sunday evenings and she'd get in her car and head back to Hanover.

Then the waiting was over, at least the first part. My activation notice arrived in the mail in August. I had a few days before I had to report, and I spent them with Marie in Hanover. From there I took a train to Boston and, at the end of August, turned myself over to the military with a bunch of other enlistees and draftees. After a couple of days in Boston they shipped us to down south to Nashville. Soon I had a proper military haircut and a uniform. Then there was a flurry of testing and processing that took about three weeks, at the end of which we were sorted out and redistributed to our proper branches of the military so they could get us up to speed.

I was assigned to the San Antonio Aviation Cadet Center, San Antonio, Texas, for basic training. I arrived around November 1. The first thing I did was sit down and write my mother and brother Bob to tell them I was getting married. I knew the Air Forces didn't like cadets to be married. It caused distractions and housing complications, among other things. But Marie and I were determined that nothing was going to stand between us before I got shipped out. Bob advised against it. He thought we should wait at least until I got my wings. But we didn't want to wait.

At the end of the year, there was a window where Marie and I could consummate our marriage plans and I had twenty-four hours of leave. She made the trip to San Antonio by rail, no small feat in those days when the trains were crammed with soldiers, sailors and airmen being moved around the country for training and dispatching. Standing-room-only was the rule in coach sections on a lot of trains, but Marie managed a club ticket and a sleeping car. My mother and my sister Jane arrived by way of Memphis with Kitty and her husband Ed Rosenwald, an ad executive based there. Bob couldn't make it, and Marie's parents couldn't be there, either, which disappointed her.

I had officially become a Protestant a couple of weeks earlier when I joined the Episcopal chapel at the Cadet Center. I really didn't differentiate between the various Protestant denominations, but the Episcopal chapel was closer than any of the others to my barracks. The pastor's name, as best I can recall, was Trenbluth, and he officiated at a crossed-swords ceremony with an honor guard on New Year's Eve, 1942. I wore my cadet's uniform, Marie a short blue dress, and she carried a bouquet of flowers. My fellow cadets sent up a cheer when we ducked under their crossed swords leaving the chapel. Our honeymoon consumed the rest of my twenty-four hour pass. We spent it at the fine old St. Anthony Hotel in San Antonio. We were happy to be starting out together, even though we didn't know what lay ahead.

The next few months were tough. We were together, but we weren't together. My ground training wrapped up around the middle of January. Then the Air Forces sent my class to Pine Bluff, Arkansas, for primary flight training. We were there for nine weeks. Marie rented a furnished room and got a job working in the Pine Bluff Arsenal while I lived in the barracks and flew open dual-cockpit trainers by Ryan (the PT-22) and Fairchild (the PT-19A). We saw each other on Sundays but there were no overnight passes for flying cadets. Around noon on days when I knew I wasn't flying, she'd come out with a sandwich and we'd hold hands and kiss each other through a chain link fence topped with barbed wire. Her regular companions were Mrs. Hutt, the landlady, and her daughter Helen, with whom Marie became close friends.

Our next stop was Coffeyville, Kansas, for basic flight training. There, the landlords were Paul and Esther Tongier and they got to be friends, too. On Sundays they loaned us their car so we could take drives in the countryside. They had nicknamed the car Squeaky, and it was. You could hear it coming from a mile away. We said goodbye to Squeaky when my old 1939 Mercury convertible arrived on a flatbed truck after I asked Bob to ship it down. Basic took another nine weeks. This time we flew a more powerful trainer called the Vultee Valiant that instructors and cadets alike called the Vultee Vibrator. These planes had one long canopy over the dual front-and-rear cockpits, and they could be covered so we could learn to fly "blind" using only instruments.

Then we were off again, this time to Pampa, Texas for advanced flight training. Now we cadets were flying twin-engine trainers, AT-9s by Curtis-Wright, AT-10s by Beechcraft, and UC-78s by Cessna. We learned to fly and land them with one engine shut down, and did more and more instrument-only flying. Mrs. Heim was our landlord in Pampa, and we became friends with a local couple, Paul and Audrey Tabor.

I will always remember these travels as a great experience. The war had brought people together, most of us at any rate. Finding a furnished room was a blood sport that pitted Marie against other cadet wives, but everywhere we went during my training everybody was just super to us. We met wonderful Americans from all walks of life. We were better off than most people in those days. A flying cadet only made $75 a month, and a furnished room cost about $25. But in 1937, when I was still in high school, my uncle Samuel Jacobs left me a $20,000 trust that produced about $800 a year. That almost doubled my Air Forces pay, and compared with most of the other cadets, especially the married ones, we were in the clover.

I got my wings on July 29, 1943. Bob came down to lend his brotherly support, but the ceremony produced some anxious moments. I knew that the top five graduates from my training class would be kept on as instructors. The lowest five would be assigned as glider pilots. The rest would be assigned to combat units, mostly in Britain at that stage of the war. When they started reading off the names, Bob told me later that Marie was clutching his hand so hard that her nails almost drew blood. She eased up when she heard my name in the top five. We were going to be together.

We were lucky in more ways than one. The planes that bombed Germany early on, without fighter protection, were easy prey for German Messerschmitts and their pilots had an 80 percent casualty rate.

Flight Instructor

It was one of those military ironies. I had completed my flight training, earned my wings, and was now a lieutenant in the U.S. Army Air Forces. But having done well enough to be tapped as an instructor, I now had to learn that job, too. That brought us back full circle. After a couple of days' leave, I got orders to report to San Antonio, this time to Randolph Field and the Central Instructors School there. Army flyers called Randolph the West Point of the Air. In my new position, Marie and I could rent our own place and live like a normal married couple.

After instructor school, which lasted about five weeks, it was right back to Pampa where I had been so recently as a student. We renewed our friendship with the Tabors, but as a rule we stuck mostly to ourselves and didn't make too many friends. Between training accidents and combat, I had already lost more friends than I cared to think about, and I didn't want to lose any more.

While we were at Pampa, somebody looked at my record and saw that I had taken French. Having taken French was a long way from speaking it, but in the heat of wartime that was a small distinction. I was told there was a group of Free French pilots at Albany, Georgia, scheduled to be trained to fly B-25s. Did I want the job?

I had flown single and multi-engine planes as a trainee and as an instructor, and found I preferred a plane that felt solid over the admittedly faster and more maneuverable fighters. My favorite plane of all was the B-25 Mitchell medium bomber. It had twin engines, machine gun stations at the nose and tail and in a bubble on the roof behind the cockpit. It could be used for strafing and bombing runs alike. Sturdy and forgiving (which made it an excellent training aircraft), the B-25 was fast becoming a stalwart of air operations throughout the U.S. military as well as a prime export to the Allied air forces. That accounted for the need to train French pilots, even though they were exiled by the German occupation and the fascist Vichy government that held sway outside the occupation zone.

I had a cousin named Jim Landauer who was serving as assistant to the commanding general of Gulf Coast Training for the Air Forces. I didn't think my French was up to the job. Nevertheless, I asked Jim what he thought and he recommended that I take it. So after a month-long detour to Selma, Alabama, where I was mistakenly assigned to instruct fighter pilots, Marie and I wound up at Turner Field in Albany, Georgia, in January 1944.

I wasn't all that fond of Albany. Marie and I found the racial attitudes there, and earlier in Selma, of a different nature altogether than we'd seen in the other places we'd been. White people seemed to actually believe that black people were on a par with children, or worse, and were therefore dismissed as a factor in all adult dealings. Our landlady was a Mrs. Rogers, and the place was the pits but with military families moving like locusts from one base to another it was all we could find.

The French pilots were willing, but not very good. Maybe it was my fault that my fractured French wasn't getting through to them. We avoided any major mishaps, though, and on the plus side I got to fly the B-25s and learned that great plane inside and out.

After awhile the French pilots were transferred to MacDill Air Base at Tampa Bay. They were given other planes to fly, and reports came up from Florida that they had a lot of accidents. "One a day at Tampa Bay" was the black humor joke among instructors.

That joke almost came back to bite me in a big way one night that August when our cadets were practicing night formations in B-25s. These were three-plane formations with one plane in front and one on each wing. The idea was to snuggle your plane up to the leader's wings and stay there. It's important to maintain your speed and direction because if you waver back and forth it gets dangerous. It was a dark night, and we were flying six planes altogether. I was flying right seat with a cadet as pilot in one formation, and my fellow instructor, a Lieutenant Greene, was doing the same thing in the other in the sky somewhere behind us.

The cadets on my left wing started having trouble keeping their plane stable so I told them to take the lead and I would get on the left wing. As I was snuggling up to the lead plane's wing, suddenly in the back of my head I saw red and green wing lights flashing. Apparently the lead cadets in the trailing formation weren't looking where they were going because they were bearing down on us fast. I keyed my radio and yelled, "Scatter!" Greene had seen what was going on and he gave the same order, signaling the cadets to break formation. For a hair-raising minute six bombers were intermingled within feet of one another, but we all landed safely and nobody was hurt. It was a miracle.

I stayed on in Albany, training pilots in B-25s throughout 1944. Early in 1945 I was chosen as one of five members of an advisory board charged with setting pilot training standards. We met once a week in offices at Turner Field and I spent the rest of the time poring over training manuals and procedures to look for ways to improve them. I did that through the end of the war and mustered out of the Army Air Forces in September 1945.

Young Parents with No Place To Go

Marie was pregnant when I left the service. We happily said goodbye to Albany and Mrs. Rogers and drove back to New York in the old Mercury convertible. September was a fine time of year for the drive. We stayed at my mother's apartment for a few days while I was summoned to a military office in Newark, New Jersey for my official discharge. It was September 25, 1945, barely five weeks after the Japanese surrendered and less than three weeks after the official surrender ceremony. I left the service as a first lieutenant. Now that the war was over, everybody could get on with their lives.

Once I had my discharge papers, I started looking for a job. I knew exactly what I wanted to do. I was going to keep flying. Commercial airlines such as Pan American, Trans World, Eastern, and American had just started to hit their stride when the war interrupted things. There were more airports now, and more people were going to be traveling by air as business resumed and people started living normally, taking vacations and visiting relatives. I was confident that all I had to do was present myself at the airline of my choice and I'd be in the cockpit in no time.

I was not the only military flyer with this thought, as it turned out. I went down to the American Airlines offices at LaGuardia Field and said, "I'm here to be an airline pilot." I was shocked when they told me to go to the end of the line. "You don't understand," I said. "I've got twenty-one hundred hours and a green instrument card." It didn't matter. I had to go to the end of the line.

The line was a long one. And there was a line just like it at every airline I applied to. It had never occurred to me that with the war finally at an end I couldn't get a job. And it was no fun living with my mother. She was nice and hospitable and perfectly pleasant about our being there, but it was a small apartment and Marie and I had no privacy. We decided to spend some time in Lake Placid while we regrouped.

By now it was early October, not long before weather you can call "crisp" in the fall turns to serious cold. The house on Buck Island was strictly a summer place. It wasn't insulated and had no central heat or running water. On top of that, it was almost a mile from the mainland, as represented by the George and Bliss Boat Landing, as the Lake Placid Marina was known then, and we were still using the outboard to get back and forth. We were isolated, there was no way I could look for a job from there, and I was miserable, consumed with worry about my future prospects.

We made it until Thanksgiving. Charlie Martin, our care-taker and onetime chaperone, worried that the lake would start to freeze and make it impossible to get back to the main-land. We swallowed our pride and moved down to Marie's parents' farm outside of Hanover. That was where we spent Christmas, 1945. I commuted between Hanover and New York as I looked for a job with increasing desperation.

The one bright moment came on January 13, 1946, when our daughter Nancy Phelan Jacobs was born at the Mary Hitchcock Hospital in Hanover. Nancy came into the world early in the morning. She was beautiful, but her arrival made me worry that much more. What are we going to do? I wondered. I've got no job and we've got no place to live.

My Unhappiest Time

The next few months were among the hardest times of my life, maybe the only time I was really unhappy. I couldn't find a job commuting back and forth, so when Nancy was only a couple of weeks old we moved back to New York and my mother's apartment. I needed to really concentrate on my job search. My mother moved out of her bedroom into the smaller second bedroom. We slept in her room and Nancy slept in the baby carriage, which there was just barely enough room for. Failing to land a job as an airline pilot and at my wit's end, I finally took a job at a retail stock brokerage

Bache and Company was its name. Its headquarters were at 36 Wall Street in the heart of the financial district, and you rode up in a private elevator. I worked in the Investment Supervisory Department for a salary of $35 a week. The clients wanted to know about dividends, and I had to look them up in a dividend book that described which stocks, common and preferred, paid what percentage dividends. I hated it, hated Wall Street, hated everything.

At the end of ninety days I couldn't take it anymore. I went to my supervisor and gave two weeks notice.

"Why are you quitting?" he said.

"I don't know," I said.

"What do you want to do?"

"I don't know."

The next day Charlie Schwartz came to my desk in the large room I shared with the other junior staff. A. Charles Schwartz was about sixty then, not a big man but a strapping athlete who had played polo and boxed as an amateur. He was the number two partner in the firm and a Wall Street veteran. Charlie had engineered the purchase of Dodge Motors from the widows of founders Horace and John Dodge and its sale to Walter Chrysler back in the 1920s when he was at Dillon Read. He'd made $15 million in the deal, lost it, and borrowed $50,000 from "Bobbie" Lehman, the legendary longtime head of Lehman Brothers, to secure a partnership in Bache. He asked me if I had a minute to see him. I followed him to a small private room and when we were there he shut the door and motioned me into a chair. He sat down himself and said, "I heard you want to quit."

"I don't think this is what I want to do," I said.

"But you don't know what you do want to do."

"I guess not," I admitted.

"You're the most mixed up kid I ever saw," he said. "You stay right here. Give it nine months. If you still don't like it after nine months, then go ahead and quit. But with Wall Street, you have the whole world at your fingertips. You'll see if you give yourself some time." Then he stood up and opened the door. The meeting was over.

Bache: Warming To Wall Street

Without other prospects, I stayed on. And in much less than nine months, I could see that he was right. They started to let me be creative, and I started to enjoy myself. I got involved in different things and found them interesting. At the time, Bache was dealing exclusively with individuals, and I could see the possibilities of developing more institutional business with small banks, mutual funds, and life insurance companies. I asked if I could explore some leads along these lines. They said fine, do it.

But when I wanted to go call on some banks up in the Adirondacks, where I could draw on a lifetime of family connections, my Bache bosses nixed the idea. There's no business there, they said.

I didn't believe it. In small towns, people didn't want to do business with a broker. They did business through their banks, where they had relationships and they were comfortable. So I decided I would do it on my own.

In the meantime, that June of 1946 Marie and I moved out of my mother's apartment into a place of our own in Forest

Hills, in Queens. This was a huge relief. Apartments were all but impossible to find since the end of the war, and we got this place through a connection of my brother's. The address was 66-20 108th Street. It had a bedroom and a half so it was big enough for the three of us, it had a lot of trees around it, and it cost $65 a month. I could walk to the Eighth Avenue subway line, which saved a nickel.

We worked hard at saving money. When we moved in I was still making only $35 a week. In those days Wall Street was not the paycheck bonanza it later became, but with the money from Uncle Samuel's trust we just got over the hump. We drank a lot of grapefruit juice, which was cheaper than orange juice, and we used oleomargarine instead of more expensive butter. The margarine came in a plastic tub. Dairy farmers had gotten a law passed at the turn of the century prohibiting the sale of yellow-colored margarine, but the makers supplied a yellow powder that we stirred in to make it look like butter. It was all worth it. An apartment of our own was another step back on the road to happiness that had begun when I started to get the hang of things at Bache. Just having our privacy back was priceless

The summer neared an end and along came Labor Day. Marie and I got ready to drive up to Lake Placid for two weeks of vacation. A day or two before we left, a piece of mail arrived that I would have died for six months earlier. It came from Pan American World Airways. I opened the envelope with shaking hands and unfolded a letter offering me a job as a co-pilot on Pan Am. My heart jumped into my throat. I had no idea what to do. I was flying one weekend a month as a reserve in the Army Air Forces. We flew Beechcraft-built AT-10 trainers out of Roosevelt Field, and I wasn't loving it. But I could envision myself flying all over the world with Pan Am, and introducing Marie and Nancy to some of the exotic destinations on the planet. On the other hand, I was feeling really comfortable at Bache. And I had promised Charlie Schwartz I would give it nine months, and the nine months wasn't up yet.

I wrote a letter turning down the Pan Am job. But after I wrote it and signed it and sealed it in an envelope and licked the stamp, I couldn't bring myself to mail it. I carried it around in my suit pocket and agonized.

Finally it came time to leave for Lake Placid, and I still hadn't mailed the letter. We packed the car and were ready to go, and I still had it in my pocket. It wasn't until I got behind the wheel and started driving that I knew what I should do. I stopped at a street corner mailbox and dropped in the letter turning down what had once been my dream job. Then I drove with a clear conscience all the way to Lake Placid.

When the banks opened after the Labor Day weekend, I called on the Bank of Lake Placid. The Jacobs family history in the area got me in to see the president. I explained that I worked for Bache and Company, a brokerage, and said, "When you buy and sell stocks and bonds for your customers, would it be possible for me to get that business?"

"You're the first person from Wall Street who's been through here for years, at least the first one who's talked to me," he said. "Sure, you can have that business."

I got the same response every place I went. By the time I was through, I had business from fourteen small banks in the Adirondack region. Back at Bache that fall, I was well along on developing the institutional business. After nine months, I got a raise to $45 a week, which eased the financial pressure slightly. More importantly, I was opening up a new niche for the firm, one where the investments (and the commissions) were bigger than with most individual clients. It was a new revenue source, and the partners took notice.

I learned some valuable lessons in those early days, lessons that today's Wall Street would do well to renew. When I was very new to the firm, the mother of a friend of mine, a very wealthy woman, told me that she would like to do her business through Bache. When I got back to the firm that day, I strode into the partners' room. It was one long room where all the partners sat at desks, and they all had red leather chairs.

I let out a big whoop to get their attention. "I got a big one," I said.

Lawrence Bache Rossbach, Harold Bache's cousin, stood up from his desk and walked straight to me. He took me by the arm and led me to another room. "Young man," he said, "don't you know that handling people's financial affairs is a sacred trust? It's not something to crow about. Don't ever talk like that again!"

Charlie Schwartz didn't say, "I told you so," when it was clear I was going to stick around. I was grateful for that, and also for his original advice. Indeed, I respected him to the extent that he became like a father to me.

A Growing Family

Less than a year after that Labor Day vacation, on August 4, 1947, Marie gave birth to our second child, a son, at Lenox Hill Hospital in Manhattan. We named him Harry Allan Jacobs III, and to avoid the usual confusion when sons are named after their fathers we called him Terry, from the words for "three" derived from Latin.

With Terry's arrival, our once spacious apartment in Forest Hills got much smaller. But my salary and savings didn't yet support a move to larger quarters. I kept riding the subway down to the Bache offices on Wall Street and we tried to put money aside.

One weekend a couple of years later, in September 1949, Marie and I were invited to a wedding in the Westchester County town of Ardsley, north of New York City. We had been looking casually for something in the suburbs. My mother now owned the building at 64 East 55th Street in Manhattan that had housed my father's office. Its managing agents, Walter and Samuel, had an office in White Plains and we had seen a real estate agent there. He asked how much we had to spend and when I told him seventeen thousand dollars he gave me a dismissive look and sniffed, "I've got nothing in that range." He was a total snob. How much we wanted to spend was actually his second question; the first was, "What club do you want to belong to?" He annoyed me, and maybe that's why we left for the wedding in time to arrive a little early. Ardsley was one of those beautiful leafy suburbs that feed the commuter trains down to the city every morning and back at night. I pulled into a convenient gas station and I asked the guy, "Are there any real estate men in town?"

He pointed to a man crossing the street. "That's Ward Thorpe. Ask him," he said.

I called to Mr. Thorpe and he came over. I told him, "We've got fifteen minutes to look for a house before we have to be at a wedding. Can you show us something?"

He climbed into the back seat and gave some directions. "The lady just came in this morning," he said. "She's getting divorced and wants to sell. Take a right at this corner."

We drove down Powder Horn Road to the end and there, on a corner lot at No. 9, was the house of my dreams. "How much is it?" I asked.

"She wants seventeen thousand," he said.

I burst into tears and said, "We'll take it."

Marie was less impulsive. "We're not going to buy a house until we can look around," she said, putting her foot down. So we went on to the wedding, went home, and came back the next day. Mr. Thorpe took us to look at two or three more houses in the area. Marie walked through them, but I refused to get out of the car. Then we went back to Ardsley and bought that house. We moved in that December, and when the neighbors saw the moving van they came over to welcome us with plates of cookies.

Climbing the Ladder

Around this time, when I was in my late twenties, I realized that one of the coming trends on Wall Street was the growth of mutual funds. With the firm's blessing, I assembled a select list of proper funds and helped set up a new department and a framework for distributing. It was an overnight success and, more importantly, a sound investment for our customers. We also increased our brokerage business with mutual funds, brought new funds to the market as an investment banker, and over time even merged a few management companies.

By 1950, aided by growth of the mutual funds department, I was making real progress at the firm. I was earning $14,000 a year, a big improvement from the $35 a week of only four years earlier. It was shaping up as a lousy year for the firm, though, so I went to Harold Bache and said, "I don't want a raise. But I do want a quarter percent interest in the firm for nothing." And he said fine.

Harold Bache had rescued the firm from near-death in 1944, when his uncle Jules Bache, the managing partner and largest shareholder, died and the other partners had to pay out nearly $4.5 million to his heirs. The defections of some heavily invested partners worsened the firm's capital position. Jack Pershing III, the son of the famous general "Black Jack" Pershing, left and started his own firm. Cliff Michel went to Loeb Rhoades. Harold had to raise the capital to keep Bache going from a disparate group of people, including Joe Kennedy, the father of the future president. That he managed to do it was a testament both to his fund-raising skills and his dedication to the firm that had started in 1879 and that Jules reorganized under the Bache name in 1892.

My quarter of 1 percent interest in Bache and Company returned $1,250 at the end of the year. A year or two later, I had started to bring in a lot of business and I was making $16,000 a year. I made the same bargain with Harold – no raise but another quarter of a percent ownership. Again, he agreed, and I was bumped to half of 1 percent. At the end of that year, I received $2,500. But the year after that, when business had improved, I received $29,000.

Ownership was clearly preferable to working only for a salary. I pressed that objective while holding down my salary and living modestly. In 1956, after working at the firm nine years, I was made a partner and continued to increase my percentage of ownership.

Some things didn't change, however. I was thirty-five years old when I made partner, and Harold Bache was over sixty. I continued to call him Mr. Bache until one morning when he said, "You're a partner now. Don't call me Mr. Bache anymore. Call me Harold."

I answered without thinking, "Yes, sir, Mr. Bache."

Golden Times: Zürs and Beyond With Nancy and Terry

Nancy turned eleven in January, 1957, and Terry would be ten that August. As the kids had grown older, Marie and I talked constantly about the need to resist the workaholism that went hand in hand with Wall Street and its pursuit of riches and to carve out some time where we could be a family. I had decided that I wanted to go up the corporate ladder as hard and fast as I could, but I didn't want to be a stranger to my children the way my father had to me, even though it was his illness and not overwork that made him distant.

Once we had decided that we would all get away together, we discussed a variety of possibilities, and looked at travel magazines, brochures and catalogues. We finally found what we were looking for in a dude ranch catalogue. The Watkins Creek Ranch in West Yellowstone, Montana, just west of the Yellowstone National Park, had a huge variety of things to do, even water skiing. We made a reservation and that summer flew out to Salt Lake City and took a sleeper to West Yellowstone.

What fun we had! Marie and I were used to riding horses,

she more than me since she had grown up with them. But the kids loved it, too. We all swam, water skied, hiked, rode for miles up into the mountains to the Continental Divide, ate at long group tables, traveled into Yellowstone to see Old Faithful, and enjoyed the amazing scenery of the West. We were there for a month, and by the end of that time we were happy and exhausted.

That time with Marie and the kids convinced me that the ticket to sanity was to get away from the pressures of the job and reconnect with what is really important over an uninterrupted period of time. I said to Marie, "We're going to keep doing this kind of thing."

About the same time, I recalled a series of conversations with my ex-sister-in-law, Ellen Lafleur. Ellen had been married to my brother Bob for four or five unhappy years. I was just a boy at the time but I was very fond of her and we had kept in touch. After Bob, she had married a ski instructor named Rene Lafleur and spent time in the Austrian ski town of Zürs, west of Innsbruck, starting in about 1952. She had raved about it, especially the Hotel Flexen there.

Marie and I had met skiing, and spent some of our happiest moments on the slopes. We had introduced Nancy and Terry to skiing and they enjoyed it, too. The dude ranch vacation had been nice but I thought – and Marie agreed – that if we took winter holidays we could follow our passion for skiing and also expand our and the kids' horizons by building in some trips to European cities. We decided to start the following winter.

There were only two problems. Nancy and Terry were both in public school in Ardsley, and any absences during the school year entered a formula that reduced the amount of state aid the school system received. Marie solved that problem when she found a hole in the rules. It said that if a student was out of the country for more than two weeks he or she was taken off the rolls and the school's state aid was not affected. Of course, the kids had to take a lot of homework with them.

Problem Number Two was the reaction at the firm. Harold Bache raised holy hell. I had thought long and hard about how to introduce the idea that I would be away for five weeks. I decided that the first thing I should do is give him plenty of warning. So sometime around Labor Day, I sent him a note saying that I would be leaving on such-and-such a date in February and would be back on such-and-such a date in March.

"That's a long time," he said when he came to my office, holding the note in one hand and tapping it against the other.

"Yes, it is," I said. "But it's important that I spend some uninterrupted time with my family. You have my undivided attention the rest of the year." I threw in what I hoped would be a sweetener. "We're also going to visit London and Paris on this trip, and eventually some other cities. These could be cities with Bache offices, and I'd look in on them."

He reluctantly agreed, and in February 1958 the four of us left for Austria. We flew Swiss Air to Zurich. On the long night over the Atlantic it occurred to me that we were on a plane like one I might be flying if Charlie Schwartz had not helped steer me on a different path.

From Zurich we took a train into Austria at Langen, and hired a car to take us the next few miles up to Zürs through thickly falling snow. Zürs was as wonderful as Ellen had promised. The little town near the Flexen Pass bustled with European skiers, and the hotel named for the pass was a traditional gem. It only had about two dozen rooms, and to me it was like an old tramp steamer sailing through the seas. We had south-facing rooms adjoining the balcony that looked out on the pass itself. The staff and enough of the guests spoke English that we managed to communicate, and I used my limited French in emergencies. We also signed up for German lessons at the little schoolhouse in the village. And skiing, of course, was a universal language shared by everyone who was in the Austrian Alps that time of year.

Nancy and Terry were blissfully oblivious to the fact that they were an ocean and half a continent away from home. They were totally at ease, so much so that we almost had a tragedy. On our third day, Marie and I came from the slopes back to the hotel to find the staff waiting for us frantically. Nancy and Terry had gotten in a snowball fight and Terry had somehow put his hand through one of the glass windows and cut himself badly. We followed the trail of blood from the Flexen down the schoolhouse, where the local doctor kept a primitive office. It turned out that Terry had severed all the tendons in his left thumb. Dr. Sepp Muir had stitched them up and put his left hand in a cast. He said Terry could keep skiing but that the cast would need to be protected. We took him to a tailor's shop where we bought a pair of man-sized mittens, one to go over the cast.

Both Terry and Nancy had been skiing practically since they could walk. It was funny. They were so little when they started that the operator of the chair lift at Mt. Sunapee in New Hampshire had to slow it down so they could jump up into the seats. Marie and I hired a private ski instructor for all of us for one of the weeks we were in Zürs and we put them into ski school the rest of the time. Terry never missed a beat despite his cast. The day before we left Dr. Muir cut the cast off and Terry could move his thumb like nothing ever happened.

The snow kept up almost the whole time we were there. We were all skiing like Olympians by the time we left. Oh, how we loved it! It was a great experience for all of us.

From Zürs we went on to Paris and London. I kept my promise to Harold Bache, visiting the firm's offices in both cities but we also made time for the sights and the museums. One night in Paris, we got a baby sitter for the kids and went out to a nightclub where I got a lot of strange looks for the big red after-ski coat I was wearing – the opposite of Paris sophistication. We stayed at Brown's Hotel in London on the recommendation of someone we had met in Zürs. This caused some amazement when a friend in London asked where we were staying. "My God," he said when I told him. "How did you get to Brown's? It's more British than the British!"

We came home in March. Neither the world nor the firm had fallen apart in my absence. This convinced me more than ever that an annual family vacation was an absolute must. Harold Bache looked at me for several days with an air of disapproval, but that might have been my winter tan from the slopes of Zürs. I resumed building up Bache's institutional client list, and nothing more was said — that year — about my long vacation.

Wall Street Social Life

By the time I made partner I was also becoming part of the clubby world of Wall Street social life. The investment banks and the brokerage houses were like a gigantic fraternity; we all ate, drank, and laughed together. A variety of social organizations existed to serve the needs of our exuberance. The Bond Club of New York and the 25 Limited Club were among them. Kappa Beta Phi was (and is) the Wall Street honorary fraternity. Fraternity is a misnomer now that women are admitted, and while Kappa Beta Phi has a reputation as a secret society it's hard to maintain secrecy when its annual black tie dinner to induct new members is held in one of New York's hotel ballrooms.

There was nothing secret about one of my most embarrassing moments on the Wall Street social circuit. When I first started to emerge at Bache as an up-and-comer there was a young man's bond club called the Investment Association of New York, and I became one of its first presidents. We had a big black tie dinner at the Waldorf where, after a lot of missteps lining up a speaker we finally got "Wild Bill" Donovan, the head of the Office of Strategic Services during World War II that morphed into the Central Intelligence Agency.

My job as president was to make a lot of introductions, including his. That went all right, but before that I had to introduce the head table, all the people from one end of the long table to the other. I asked them all to stand and the people in the audience to hold their applause until they'd all been introduced. So I did that and when I sat down my ears were burning with embarrassment. I knew I'd done something wrong, but I couldn't figure out what it was. Then it hit me! I'd introduced everyone but Harold Bache, who was sitting about two seats away from me.

One of my friends leaned over to Mr. Bache and said, in a voice that I could hear, "Fire him in the morning." Fortunately, he didn't.

I was on the board, at different times, of the Investment Bankers Association and the Association of Stock Market Firms. These groups met at fine resorts around the country, places like the Greenbriar in West Virginia, or in different cities, invariably under great conditions since we represented things that mayors and governors covet such as markets for their bonds and the prospect of improving the performance of their pension funds. We made around four of these trips every year, and Marie always joined me.

My competitors were my close friends, people like Bill Todd from Kuhn Loeb, Bob Baldwin from Morgan Stanley, John Hilsen from Wertheim, Andy Sage from Lehman Brothers, and Wally La Tour from Dupont. There were regional firms where I struck up friendships, too. Henning Hilliard of J. J. B. Hilliard in Louisville; Wheelock Whitney, the CEO of J. M. Dain in Minneapolis; Jack Hagan from Mason Hagan in Richmond – I shared interests and concerns with all these men, and they, too, were part of the fraternity.

Only later would Wall Street open up to women who would add grace, wit, and moderating influences to this so-called fraternity.

The Start of My Political Conversion

Growing up on Wall Street I was of course a Republican. Everybody else was, so why not me? I had voted for Eisenhower over Stevenson in 1952 and 1956 with great enthusiasm. I voted for Nixon over Kennedy in 1960, too, although that may have had more to do with some distaste I had for Kennedy's father than any fondness for Dick Nixon.

What happened with Joe Kennedy went back to Harold Bache's desperate fight to keep the firm going after his uncle Jules died and he needed to raise capital. Kennedy had put in $500,000 and was a limited partner, with what percentage of ownership I don't know. The firm had strict rules that governed adjustments to their capital and their percentage of the profits. One was that these partners had to notify the firm by September 30 if they wanted to add or remove capital by February 1 of the following year and change their partnership percentage. So one day the phone rang — it was after September 30 of whatever year it was, probably 1949 or 1950 — and it was Joe Kennedy calling Harold Bache. He demanded that his percentage of the profits be increased by

20 percent. And Harold said, "Well, it's after September 30 and anyhow, Joe, we shook hands." And Joe Kennedy said, in effect, "Well, that's too bad. This is the way it is and I don't care whether we shook hands or not." Harold really needed the capital then. But he said, "Joe, if that's the way you feel I think it's best if you take your money out and we part ways." So he was a tough guy but he pulled out of the firm when Harold put his foot down.

But anyway, Nixon lost and the party started to change. In 1964, Marie and I decided to take the children out to the Republican convention in San Francisco. John Roosevelt, FDR's youngest son, was a Bache partner and a Republican, an odd twist on his father's thoroughly Democratic legacy. I went out with him early to go to some committee meeting and then I was going to meet Marie and the kids out there. Well, John and I went to this meeting and the discussion turned to the United Nations and Eleanor Roosevelt, who had died only two years earlier. She had been a big U.N. supporter. And people got up and hissed when they heard her name! Can you imagine that? John was furious. He got up and walked out and came back to New York.

New York Senator Jacob Javits had gotten us our convention tickets. I knew Jack well and admired him. He had been re-elected in 1962 to his second term and he was a good friend to New York. But he was from the liberal wing of the party, and conservatives were rebelling against the so-called "Wall Street Republicans" who were fiscally conservative but socially moderate and for whom pragmatism governed foreign policy. Our tickets showed that the conservatives had taken over. They were the worst in the house, way up and in the back of the Cow Palace. We were there the night Nelson Rockefeller gave a speech denouncing extremism, and they booed him off the floor. It was ugly, and I'll never forget it.

If I had needed further persuasion, Barry Goldwater's speech accepting the Republican nomination practically called for bombing Vietnam back to the Stone Age. I voted for

Lyndon Johnson that November, and was well along the path of my political conversion.

I went further still a little later, in 1967. Bache had acquired a New York financial services firm that went by the name of its owner, Richard J. Buck. Buck was an intimate friend of Richard Nixon, who was plotting his political comeback after his defeat in 1960 and losing to Pat Brown in the California governor's race in 1962. After Nixon joined the Mudge Rose law firm in New York, Buck asked the firm to arrange a luncheon to introduce Nixon to the financial community.

Harold Bache asked me to put the lunch together, but on the day it was scheduled, after Nixon had arrived at our offices, I got a call from his secretary saying that Mr. Bache was sick. Could I take over and make the introductions? I took Nixon around and then we went to the India House Club for lunch with eighteen or so senior partners at some of the major Wall Street firms including Merrill Lynch, Morgan Stanley and Kuhn Loeb.

After that, Buck brought in his client John Shaheen, an entrepreneur with Lebanese roots who had worked for the OSS during the war monitoring oil flows to Axis nations. Shaheen owned oil and petrochemical businesses around the world. Now he had won – some said through bribes -- the backing of the premier of Newfoundland, Canada, to build a refinery on the coast in a little town called Come-By-Chance. He laid out his $200 million plan at a meeting with Buck, Nixon, Harold Bache, me, and Peter Danes, who was in charge of investment banking. Danes was a Czech refugee who had come to the United States after the war. I finally had a lunch with Dick Buck at which I suggested we weren't the right fit for Shaheen's plan. I said he needed a major investment bank with an oil industry component such as Lehman Brothers, and I heard no more about the deal.

None of this improved my view of Nixon. Dick Buck was also acting as an investment banker for a company called Transcontinental Investing, which among other things was into record distribution. He had been going around buying other, smaller distribution companies. By early 1968, Transcontinental Investing had become of one of the top rack-jobbers – distributors who sold records to non-traditional outlets like drugstores and supermarkets – with $80 million a year in sales. When Harold Bache died in March 1968, these companies started calling up and demanding to know where the cash was that Buck had promised them. It turned out that he had been using Transcontinental Investing stock to buy these companies but promising that if they didn't want it, Bache would buy it from them for a fixed price. He had committed some $18 million, and had signed the documents as if he was acting for Bache.

We consulted Arthur Dean, then the head of the famous Wall Street law firm Sullivan and Cromwell. His response was vivid: "We need to tear off his epaulets and break his sword."

Bill Goldenblum from Bache's law department and I headed down to St. Croix in the U.S. Virgin Islands to do just that. We left on April 4, 1968 and arrived late at night to the news that Dr. Martin Luther King Jr. had been assassinated. After a few hours of sleep, we sat down with Dick Buck over breakfast and told him Bache would not be redeeming Transcontinental Investing shares for cash and that our relationship with him was over.

I suppose we could have gotten sued. But Lyndon Johnson had just announced he wouldn't run again in the face of opposition to the war in Vietnam. The stock market rose in gratitude, lifting Transcontinental Investing's shares on the Amex above the level Buck had promised from Bache, and the issue, and Dick Buck, went away.

There was a level of sleaziness about these people that I just couldn't stand. Their deals were worth millions but they acted like small-time hustlers trying to get over on the next guy for a few hundred bucks. Their concept of honor was winning, and it didn't matter how. My conversion was almost complete.

Family Time

Marie and I had continued our winter trips to Zürs with Nancy and Terry. They were helping us build a family memory bank that I knew would outstrip any recollections I might have had of goings-on on Wall Street that I missed while we were skiing.

At the beginning, as I said, Harold Bache raised holy hell. I kept up the practice I had used that first year, sending him a note every Labor Day saying that I was leaving on February so-and-so and that I'll be here and here and here and I'll be back on such and such a date. He used to complain that it was a long time to be gone. One year in January he sent a note around saying there would be a partners' meeting in the middle of February to study incorporation. We were a partnership at that point. He said it was "a vital meeting." I wrote back saying I was going to miss that meeting and enclosed a copy of my memorandum from Labor Day. So he blew his stack. He said, "You better change your schedule."

I said, "No, I'm not going to. I have a limited time to be with my wife and children and I'm not changing."

So we went to Zürs as usual and added two cities with Bache offices and then we came home. I got back to the office and learned that the "vital" meeting had blown up. Nobody could agree and nothing had happened.

I said to Mr. Bache, "I guess it didn't matter that I was gone, then. Nothing was accomplished."

"If you were here something might have been," he said.

The firm deferred the question of incorporation for a while. I knew it would eventually happen, because as a corporation we would be able to build up capital while as a partnership we paid out the earnings every year. In the interim, Mr. Bache softened his attitude about my trips. "You know, you were right to do that, to do things with your children" he said. "So many people I know on Wall Street, they just worked all the time and never got to know their families. You did, and it took a lot of discipline to do that."

We did have some times to remember, and friends to cherish. Early on, we met Willi Böckle. Willi was the poor son of a railroad worker in the valley below Zürs who worked his way through architecture school, then got hold of some land in Zürs and put up a little hotel. He also worked as a ski instructor just because he loved it. Willi and his wife also had some property in southern Austria, in Klagenfurt. With his various interests, he had become a millionaire. Marie and I got along famously with him, and he became one of the closest friends I ever had.

Embraced by the wonderful camaraderie at Zürs and traipsing around the cities we visited, Nancy and Terry developed an early sophistication about European ways and people and learned from their young friends to speak German fluently. Later each of them spent time in Germany during their summer vacations.

It may sound as if these family vacations were extravagant, five weeks in Europe every winter, but I did my best to instill some lessons about thrift along the way. My rule for our *après ski* moments was that the kids could have one treat only. They could have either hot chocolate or a piece of cake, but not both. I kept this rule in place even after Nancy and Terry were married and had kids of their own who came to Zürs on our family trips, and Marie and I always followed it ourselves. And when it came to meals, the Jacobs family rarely if ever ordered from the expensive side of the menu. I like a good steak as much as the next person, but I've never bought into the idea that you can't have a perfectly good meal for much less money and, that being the case, that's what you should do. Maybe that's because I grew up during the Depression, an experience later generations can't appreciate.

I also learned a lot, sometimes about my overseas Bache colleagues. The first time we included Rome in our itinerary I called the manager of the Bache office there. His name was Count Fernando Pecci-Blunt, and his friends called him Dino. In my opinion he was an ass, a real stuffed shirt. His father, the son of a successful German Jewish leather merchant who came to the United States in the nineteenth century, had changed his name from Blumenthal to Blunt. He was a count because his father had married a countess named Pecci, who was the niece of Pope Leo XIII. Dino had known Jack Kennedy at Harvard and had entertained Jackie Kennedy and her sister at his villa in Rome. I called him up and said, "I'm Harry Jacobs, and I'm the syndicate manager and I'm in Rome and I wonder if you can have tea with us tomorrow at 5 o'clock." And he said, "No."

A warmer snapshot from our excursions was an Ash Wednesday audience with Pope John XXIII. We were part of a large group but it was very exciting for the kids. Another time, we visited Milan and after stopping at the Bache office there we drove down through the mountains into France and found a village called Villefranch sur Mer on the coast between Monaco and Nice. We had all heard about the French Riviera, which made the Welcome Hotel in Villefranch all the more surprising and attractive – it was twelve dollars a day with meals!

We also got lessons in European history. We visited Madrid in the days not long after the fascist head of state, Generalissimo Francisco Franco, died in 1975. The new head of the Bache office at the time was a member of Franco's nationalist party, the far-right fascist wing of it, and he took us to meet a guy who had been a financial advisor to Franco. His name was March. This guy hadn't stopped at Franco; he had a big picture on his office wall of Hermann Göring, the Nazi commander of the Luftwaffe during World War II who had practiced by bombing anti-fascist villages during the Spanish Civil War. It was scary that such a level of attachment to fascism still existed after Franco's death.

By then, Nancy and Terry weren't with us nearly so often. Once they graduated from high school, Nancy in 1964 from Ardsley High School and Terry a year later from the Holderness School in New Hampshire, their class and activity schedules at Smith and Dartmouth, respectively, made it hard to block out the time I had originally insisted on.

It was just such a conflict that delayed our trip to Zürs from February until mid-March, 1968. I had lunch with Mr. Bache and Henry Watts, then the chairman of the New York Stock Exchange, on March 14. We were leaving for Austria that night, and I excused myself early in order to go home and pack. Instead of saying goodbye to Harold Bache, for some reason I said instead, "God bless you."

We arrived in Zürs the next day following our usual route, Swiss Air to Zurich, the train to Langen, a car to Zürs. We had a pattern that we followed. We'd check in at the Flexen and I'd go down and take the skis out of the bag and we'd put on our boots and skis and take one or two quick runs on the baby hill. I was downstairs taking the skis out when Marie came running to get me to the telephone. Harold Bache had gone to sleep the night before and never woke up. So we came tearing back to New York.

Bache: Scramble at the Top

I was one of four executive vice presidents of Bache and Company when Harold Bache died unexpectedly. It wasn't exactly as if he'd died without a will, but close. Because he had told me I was going to be president but he never told anybody else. And while my record at the firm was overwhelmingly positive, I had made at least one misstep that might have undermined my chances.

In 1965, when I was managing the syndicate department, I had received a call from the legendary fund manager Jerry Tsai. He said he was leaving Fidelity Funds to start a new growth fund and wanted to tell me what he had in mind. He was going to be in New York the next day and we arranged to have lunch. I took along Chuck Rendig, the assistant syndicate manager, and Jack Jansing, the manager of the mutual fund department. Tsai's plan sounded good, and that afternoon we got executive committee approval to bring him on. Within a few weeks he had raised almost $400 million, which was a lot of money in those days. But Tsai did a poor job of investing and our customers lost money. We should never have entrusted our clients' money to him.

Still, I was clearly committed to the firm and its prospects. Bache had finally converted from a partnership to a corporation in 1965. I had continued to increase my percentage of ownership, topping out at 3 percent by means of some serious borrowing totaling some $250,000. Altogether I had about $700,000 in the firm when Harold Bache died.

There was some confusion at first about the succession. George Weiss, who had been at Bache for many years, became chairman of the board but because he was seventy-three years old took on no additional duties. The three contenders to actually run the firm were John Leslie, the Austrian-born lawyer and accountant who chaired the executive committee; Robert C. Hall, the company treasurer who was also an executive vice president; and me. John Leslie was 57, Bob Hall was 52, and I was 47.

By the second week in April the board had agreed on an executive and operating structure that would run without a CEO. Weiss continued as board chairman and *eminence gris*. Leslie, who had come to the United States before the war, became the chief administrative officer. Hall remained treasurer and added the title of chief financial officer. I was the new president.

Ironically, this corporate structure was announced at about the same time Merrill Lynch was restructuring, with Donald T. Regan named the president there. We were the two largest investment firms in the world at the time, although Merrill Lynch had more than twice our 6,000 employees and about fifty more than our 124 offices. Don Regan, of course, would go on to serve as secretary of the treasury under Ronald Reagan and later was his chief of staff. I admired him at Merrill Lynch, but not in the government.

As executive vice president, I had been in charge of investment banking, institutional clients and trading, indeed most of the outside operations that boiled down to the fact that my job was increasing the firm's business. I would remain over those areas as president, and would also propose and review the company's key policies and practices. This last part was very important. I had been at Bache now for twenty-two years, and believed the Bache reputation for integrity had to be protected and preserved.

I had a delicious moment of personal revenge soon after I was elected the firm's president. I got a call one day from Count Pecci-Blunt, the head of the Rome office who had snubbed my invitation to tea when we were there a few years earlier. He said, "Mr. Jacobs, I'm in New York for a few days and I wonder if I could come to see you." And I said, "Sure, that's no problem. Be in my office at five of twelve tomorrow. We can talk. By the way, I have a twelve o'clock lunch date."

A year later, in April 1969, I announced at the Bache annual meeting that John Leslie had been elected chairman. There was still no chief executive, at least officially, but John's chairmanship embraced executive responsibility. I worked well with him and we had Austria in common, but the rivalries over his eventual successor would become intense.

Turmoil on Wall Street

Storm clouds were gathering over Wall Street in the late 1960s. The business was changing. Investors chastened by the example of the crash of 1929 had for a long time bought stocks and held them, happy to collect dividends and realize gradual price appreciation. But inflation fears took hold in the 1960s, causing both individual and institutional investors to turn over stocks more quickly. Volume increased to the point where, in those days before computers, firms could not process their business. The whole machinery broke down. The biggest problem was the "fail." Brokerage firms had five days to deliver stocks they had sold, and they couldn't do it. Some of them couldn't do it for a month.

It all came to a head in 1968. In January, the New York Stock Exchange and the Amex started shutting down at two in the afternoon instead of the usual three-thirty to give their back offices a chance to catch up on their paperwork. This failed to solve the problem, and in June the major exchanges adopted a four-day week, closing on Wednesdays. By then almost fifty firms were under restrictions imposed by the Securities and

Exchange Commission for their high volume of fails. The exchanges still couldn't shovel themselves out from under the paperwork deluge, and in November they agreed to trade for just four hours a day, from ten to two, starting in January 1969. For all of the cutbacks in trading time, market volume in 1968 was the highest ever.

Bache was less affected by these problems than most other firms. This was a credit to John Leslie, who had recognized the need for efficient back office operations early on. And in 1968 he brought in a very capable back office guy named Frank A. Digitaeno with the title vice president and controller. Together they maintained our operations capability and we had no trouble processing transactions and responding to our clients.

That same year, John made a brilliant move. The economy and back office problems were battering Wall Street, and everyone was looking to save money. The Tishman real estate company had some property on Gold Street near the Brooklyn Bridge where it wanted to put up an office building. I don't know what our per-square-foot rents were at 36 Wall Street, but Tishman dangled the Gold Street space for $5.50 a square foot. In June, John committed to leasing six floors and moving our operations and accounting staffs to the new building. He also ordered a new computer system for $3.5 million. The executive offices, investment banking, sales, research and general administration were supposed to stay behind, but John ended up moving the entire firm – front and back offices and data processing -- to Gold Street in 1969. Everybody was complaining, especially the investment bankers, but it was the right thing to do and a move that, because of my outside focus on sales and bringing in new business, I never could have pulled off.

Elsewhere on Wall Street, there were shotgun mergers, financial collapse, and panics. Several old-line firms died or were absorbed in those rough days, most because they were partnerships without the permanent capital that incorporation would have given them. Francis I. DuPont lost its independence and merged with Glore Forgan in 1970. Hayden Stone was taken over. Hornblower & Weeks survived in name only, and Gregory and Goodbody, two more old Wall Street names, disappeared entirely. W. E. Hutton also disappeared.

In the midst of this turmoil, in April 1969, I was elected to the board of governors of the New York Stock Exchange. My election brought to fruition a conversation I had had years earlier with Jim Kellogg, who had chaired the NYSE at a very early age. He was only 36 when he was appointed to chair the board of governors in 1951. Before that, in 1936 when he was 21, he had become the youngest seat holder on the exchange. Spear Leeds & Kellogg was (and is) one of the invaluable firms that specialize in getting transactions on the exchange executed and cleared, loaning stocks when needed to fulfill commitments others have made. Jim and his wife had four sons, and he was a very dynamic guy and one of my favorite people. We were having lunch when the subject of my going on the NYSE board of governors came up. I don't know who raised the subject, but I said, "What do I have to do?"

"Shut up and don't do anything," he said.

That was the way Jim ran meetings, as I learned later when he chaired the Association of Stock Exchange Firms. Every meeting went boom, boom, boom, with never any discussion. He was a very capable guy, but sitting still and doing nothing wasn't possible in the conditions affecting the New York Stock Exchange when I went on the board. Doing business four hours a day allowed the exchange and financial firms to keep up with their paperwork, but it curtailed the business of capital formation, which spawns new business, jobs, and an expanding economy.

The first thing that was clear to me was that the exchange needed to go back to longer hours. Firms had started hiring operations personnel at a much higher rate than sales staff. They were spending millions on automation. The exchange could keep the pressure on. I argued that if you have a big factory it makes no sense to keep it open just a few hours a day. You have machinery and personnel in place, and it's more efficient to keep them on the job.

Bernard J. "Bunny" Lasker was the NYSE chairman when I started my term. Robert W. Haack was its president. The latter was a full-time paid job. By that summer, the SEC had concurred with us and the American Exchange that we should expand the trading day by half an hour. It was an experiment. The exchange would drop the extra thirty minutes if the paperwork problems worsened again. In July 1969 the NYSE and the Amex started to close at two-thirty.

The paperwork avalanche had started to subside. By May 1970, after an interim expansion of another half an hour, the exchanges resumed their normal trading hours of ten in the morning to three-thirty in the afternoon.

That wasn't my only crusade as a member of the NYSE board of governors, but I'm proud to say I was the leading architect for longer hours.

My Political Conversion Is Complete

Bunny Lasker was one of the many Wall Streeters who was very fond of Richard Nixon. He had raised money for Nixon's successful 1968 campaign, in which Nixon succeeded Lyndon Johnson and promised to end the war in Vietnam. I had voted for Hubert Humphrey after changing my party registration to Democratic in 1967. I think Humphrey would have ended the war. Nixon expanded it instead.

You could blame both political parties for Vietnam. Kennedy had gotten us into it with Cold War thinking. Johnson had listened to the same Cold War arguments in escalating the American commitment. Nixon ended the draft and brought in a lottery to replace it, but his pledge of "peace with honor" had some strange components including the bombing of Cambodia that stretched out the war for five more years during the snail-like Paris peace talks.

I had gotten to know LBJ's last secretary of defense, Clark Clifford, over many years of consultation about goings-on in Washington that affected the financial world. Our relationship started when Harold Bache was still alive. He thought we ought to have a representative in Washington. Clark also represented Merrill Lynch but Mike McCarthy, who chaired Merrill at the time, told Harold it was fine if we also wanted to use Clark, too. Harold was too busy to go down to check on pending legislation, so I used to go down about once a month to sit with Clark and find out what was what. And we gradually got to be good friends.

He'd sit there and make his hands into steeples and then he'd tell me about experiences he'd had, like when he was an aide to Harry Truman and the architect of his campaign against Tom Dewey that nobody thought Truman could win. He was instrumental in persuading Truman to recognize Israel over the objections of General George C. Marshall, the author of the Marshall Plan. Later, when he replaced Robert McNamara as LBJ's secretary of defense he saw that the war was tearing the country apart and started the ball rolling to withdraw from Vietnam before Nixon got in and screwed it up. We had a lot of conversations during that time when I was questioning my political affiliation and I asked Clark why he was a Democrat. He said they just do more for more people. They pressed for civil rights legislation, for example. They created Medicare so our older population had their health care needs met. And the Republicans were moving more and more to the right.

Nancy had graduated from Smith College in the spring of 1968. Terry was due to graduate from Dartmouth in the spring of 1969, and unlike his sister he faced being drafted and sent to Vietnam. We had always had the kind of relationship where we could talk, and Terry said he wasn't going. He said he would rather go to Canada, although I'm not sure he really meant it.

I was an old Air Force jock, but I thought it over and I told him, "Nixon is a rotten president and this is a rotten war. Whatever you do I'll back you one hundred percent even if you go to Canada."

What he did instead was join Volunteers in Service to America. VISTA was part of Lyndon Johnson's War on Poverty, a domestic Peace Corps that put young volunteers like Terry into low-income areas to fix some of the problems. He ended up working with an activist United Methodist minister, the Rev. Ken Crossman, to help found and run a program for black unwed mothers in Davie, Florida, a poor area west of Fort Lauderdale. That lasted until the lottery replaced the draft and he drew a high number that meant he wouldn't be called. I could not have been more proud of him.

VISTA was another invention of the Democrats. It demonstrated yet again the party's progressive, humanistic thrust. That impulse would be muted by Nixon's "Southern Strategy" aimed at remaking the Democratic "solid South" into a whites-dominated Republican stronghold, and pilloried by Ronald Reagan as he cut taxes and steered money from the poor to the rich. But it was programs like VISTA that gave young people like Terry an option to the war that made me determined to cast my lot with the Democrats from now on.

I have to add one caveat with regard to Nixon: John Leslie had been the honorary Austrian consul-general in New York. He was a Nixon supporter and I knew he yearned to be the ambassador to his native country, so at some point I gave Nixon $1,000 toward his next campaign to help John's cause. I got a tie tack in return. Nancy and Terry were furious. They let me know about it on the Christmas morning after I'd given the donation. Down at the toe of my stocking hanging on the mantle piece, along with a sooty lump of coal, was the Nixon tie tack. We laughed about that for days.

New Houses

We had lived in Ardsley for twenty golden years by 1969. The children grew up, my career blossomed, and we started to take those long winter vacations that we all treasured. Our house on Powder Horn Road was a modest one, with two bathrooms and four bedrooms. The money we had saved by not buying a grand house had gone into our vacations. But after I became president of Bache, money was less of a consideration. And now the block was getting younger and drawing lower income families. Two policemen had houses up the street. At the same time I was having to entertain more, and needed more space for parking. It was time to move.

Marie and I had talked about living on the Hudson River. We asked one of our neighbors, a real estate broker, to look for something. He found a beat-up fifties-style ranch house about ten minutes away in Irvington. We looked at it and fell in love.

Irvington is a little bedroom town right on the river. Its Main Street climbs up from the Metro North train station. The rail line runs along the river, and even some of the town benches along Main Street have river views. The house was in Matthiessen

Park, a community of nice houses on big lots high on a bluff. It sat near the brow of the bluff where the land sloped down, and it had a terrace that gave magnificent views of the river. It even had a little kidney-shaped swimming pool, which was the style of the time. There were other bidders, and I kept telling our broker, "Pay more." We bought it for $140,000 and added at least $10,000 with Marie's extensive restoration. We moved in over the Labor Day weekend in 1969.

It was our second new home in about a year. We had decided we wanted to spend more time at Lake Placid, and maybe even visit in the winter. We both remembered that fall after the war, when we stayed until Thanksgiving in the unwinterized family house on Buck Island, huddling in blankets at night until the threat of ice on the lake forced us to leave. Now we wanted the choice to stay or go to be our own and not leave it up to the quirky North Country weather.

About this time a two-bedroom camp on the mainland came on the market. It was on a peninsula just across from the family compound, a short boat ride of less than half a mile. It cost $28,000 and the *pièce de résistance*, a 1958 22-foot Chris Craft runabout with a 165-horsepower Chrysler marine engine, came with it. I have never cared all that much for material things, but that boat, christened "White Cloud" like the house, is an exception.

The house, with a boathouse underneath so you could come in off the lake and walk upstairs, wasn't winterized at first. That was one of the first things we did. Then Marie and I would come up early in December and again after Christmas through New Years. We were still going to Austria in February and March, but we'd also come to Lake Placid to catch a late week of spring skiing. Later, after Terry finished his stint in VISTA and went on to architecture school at Penn, under his guidance we expanded the place in all directions. Nevertheless, even with seven rooms it's still a simple house with great charm, open all year round, and a source of happiness for all the family. I still spend three and a half months or more there every year.

Bache: Going Public

The record volume of transactions in 1968 had overwhelmed Wall Street's back offices. The end of 1968 brought an end to the bull market LBJ had started by announcing he wouldn't run again. Stock prices fell in 1969 and volume fell with them, cutting commission revenues. From coping with too much paperwork and spending heavily to address the problem, now Wall Street was suffering from too little income.

John Leslie had added to Bache's overhead to stay ahead of the transactions the firm had to process. Now he had to reverse course. His actions echoed a saying of Harold Bache's. "Bache's risk is in its overhead," he said, adding that for a firm like Salomon Brothers the risk was in its product inventory. In 1969 we closed branch offices, laid off staff, and cut salaries and bonuses. The firm still lost almost $5 million in the fiscal year ending January 31, 1970, and $2.5 million the next year. In the first four months of 1970 we laid off 30 percent of our staff.

All this produced huge pressure on me to increase sales. It put pressure on the firm as well. For a retail brokerage like

Bache, there were few sources of income outside turnover, and Bache was not a firm that "churned" its customers' stock just to collect commissions. But there was another option only recently available to Wall Street.

I was on the NYSE board of governors when Donaldson, Lufkin & Jenrette, a relatively young investment banking firm, came to the board with a proposal that rocked the Wall Street boat. It wanted to go public, against the longstanding rules of the stock exchange. Bunny Lasker was against it. He yelled and screamed at Danny Lufkin, who had come to press his case and force the exchange's hand. But the governors narrowly approved the public offering. I was one of those who favored it. DLJ sold its first shares in April, 1970, and showed the member firms of the exchange that they had a new fundraising option. Merrill Lynch followed suit the following summer.

Following the Merrill Lynch offering by one month, Bache announced at the end of July 1971 that we would make an initial public offering of 2.5 million shares. By that time, the exchange had imposed a commission surcharge of $15 or 50 percent of the regular commission, whichever was smaller, to help its member firms return to profitability, and Bache was in the black again.

The offering, on September 16, was successful. The syndicate of underwriters led by First Boston set a price of $16 for the shares. The offering was oversubscribed but not by a lot; shares traded for as high as $16.75 during the day but closed at the $16 offering price. It brought in $40 million that we would use primarily to reduce outstanding debt and stabilize our capital situation. The main thing, however, was that our capital was now permanent. That was a huge relief. Many firms that didn't have permanent capital would disappear in the next few years.

Bache: Fighting for the Top Spot

The first half of the 1970s bought out intense rivalries at Bache. These focused, naturally, on who would succeed John Leslie as the chief executive. I thought it should be me.

My first rival was Bob Hall. He was an attractive guy, very upper crust. He had degrees from Harvard and Oxford and had worked at Guaranty Trust before moving to Bache. And he was Harold Bache's fair-haired boy. He and his wife saw a great deal of the Baches socially. When Harold Bache died he was the firm's treasurer, chaired the finance committee, and was one of the four executive vice presidents.

I liked Hall well enough. He was an amiable guy. But from what I had seen he faded in the clinches. What I mean by that, he didn't like to face up to bad news and could have gotten us into exposed financial positions by failing to confront realities. I recognized this while Harold Bache was still alive.

I told Harold, "You know, I have all my money in here, every penny, and if Bob Hall were CEO I would worry about control and supervision." I had in mind the kind of nightmare scenarios that occurred at Bear Stearns and Lehman in the

2008 financial crisis, though I didn't imagine anything that bad. I said, "If he becomes CEO, I'm out." So he was on notice.

Of course, after Harold died unexpectedly, Bob Hall's name cropped up in speculation about who would succeed him, along with John Leslie and me. Once John was elected chairman and assumed the CEO's duties, Bob remained a contender. But he still had that habit of not dealing with bad news.

One example came up right after Harold died. At the time we were involved with Dick Buck and Transcontinental Investing but had not yet learned that Buck had promised Bache would pay cash for the Transcontinental Investing shares he had used to buy his rack-jobbing record distributors. Bob Hall let Buck name him to the TI board, the lone outside board member along with three insiders. It was a bad situation, an invitation to disaster, and he should never have accepted it.

Later on, I got a letter from some people I call copper junkies. They were scrap copper traders who were using copper futures to offset their risk. Their letter claimed we had harmed them somehow in our commodities department, and they threatened to sue. I passed it on to Hall but he didn't deal with the problem. He just put the letter in a drawer. I think we eventually were sued, and lost.

Hall faded as a candidate under John Leslie's leadership and he left the firm eventually. But another rival emerged. This was Frank Digaetano, an accountant who had been a partner at Arthur Andersen before coming to Bache in 1968. John liked him because he, like John, was a very able back office guy who placed a lot of emphasis on operations. He helped engineer our move to Gold Street and was one of the reasons we stayed ahead of the paperwork problems that affected so many other firms in the late 1960s and early 1970s.

By 1974, the year after Bache acquired the investment banking firm Halsey Stuart and became Bache Halsey Stuart, Digaetano's role was expanding and he was being suggested in the business press as a possible candidate for CEO. He was named vice chairman. In my view he had no presence, and looked like a back office guy, meaning he had no smiles and no personality, and he wouldn't have worked as CEO. But I still figured that I had to finish him off.

As a public company, we had an outside compensation committee to set executive compensation including stock options. The stock sold for as low as $2.75 in 1974 but in 1975 it recovered and the compensation committee was awarding stock options. At one meeting they gave John Leslie options for 40,000 shares. The committee decided at a second meeting a few weeks later to give me 15,000 options and Digaetano 10,000 options. Digaetano objected. He said he wanted more options, and in fact he wanted more options than me. He kept complaining about it, which I thought was kind of stupid.

Finally I hit on a solution that hurt me in the short run but would help in the long run. Appearing before the compensation committee, I said, "Frank, you take as many options as you want and I'll take none." And he was stupid enough to say okay. That did him in because later on when his options grab became public in our proxy statements and other filings, the rest of senior management was ready to kill him. And I got my options anyway. I knew he was finished. His candidacy faded along with his popularity.

A Footnote:

Our Halsey Stuart purchase provided a footnote to one of the big names on Wall Street. This was Peter G. Peterson, the former U.S. Secretary of Commerce and then Lehman Brothers CEO who would later co-found the private equity powerhouse The Blackstone Group. It had to do with tombstones, as bond advertising in the newspapers was known. Tombstones were divided between first-tier and second-tier firms. Halsey Stuart was first-tier, Bache second-tier. Within their categories, firms' ads appeared in alphabetical order, as in Blyth, First Boston,

Halsey Stuart, Lehman Brothers, and so on. But a couple of years after we bought Halsey Stuart, we dissolved the name as a division of Bache and switched to the Bache name. That meant we now were near the front of the alphabetical listings in the first tier, which caused some jealousies. The way I heard the story, somebody went in and told Peterson, "Bache wants to appear as Bache, which will put them ahead of us in the tombstone advertising." And Peterson reportedly said, "Don't bother me with that nonsense. Just do it." I saw him as a very incisive, no-nonsense leader.

Another footnote to this story is that with the advent of the Internet such advertising in newspapers no longer exists.

New CEO

John Leslie knew after Digaetano's options *faux pas* that the candidates to succeed him had narrowed down pretty much to one. In the late summer of 1975, John had accepted the chairmanship of the National Market Advisory Board, a group that advised the Securities and Exchange Commission on market regulation. Soon afterward, he approached me to suggest that it was time to elevate me to CEO.

As hard as I had labored for that day, I had to tell him that I disagreed. I thought it was a question of timing. I felt that my end of the business, the production and marketing end, was in good shape. But we still faced hurdles in the area where John was at his best, organizational planning, and I didn't think the firm could lose him then. In a memo to him dated September 15, 1975, I suggested among other things that Frank Digaetano, as chief financial and chief operating officer, look at electronic data processing and other operational areas to reduce our overall cost of doing business, and that we hire one of the business services and consulting firms such as Arthur Anderson or Coopers Lybrand to study our overall cost structure with an eye to cutting our expenses. I concluded, "With management efforts being directed at both corporate reorganization and financial streamlining, it would seem to me a most inappropriate time for me to take over the reins of C.E.O."

I did say I would "take over as quickly as possible as many of your principal jobs as possible. This can include responsibilities both ceremonial and unpleasant."

I envisioned the transition taking place a year or more later, in November, 1976, or after his return from Europe that August. "If that compromise is not satisfactory," I wrote, "I would reluctantly go along with becoming C.E.O. on my 55th birthday, June 28, 1976. I have now thought long and carefully about this and <u>respectfully advise that this is the earliest date which I think is in the interest of the firm for me to take over.</u> Bache & Co. needs your top leadership for these extra few months."

He responded the next day in a memo that, as I look back on it, seemed disappointed and perplexed. "With respect to the Chief Executive Officer matter, I cannot follow your reasoning. I don't agree on certain premises as stated and don't believe the conclusions are applicable.

"Regardless of all that, however, as a practical matter, I have to accede to your wishes that you do not want to take on the assignment as Chief Executive Officer at this time. I therefore will continue my responsibilities."

Why did I refuse to take the brass ring when it was within my grasp? In addition to the need for John to stay on and concentrate on enhancing the all- important areas that included Bache's law department as well as EDP and operations, I had a personal agenda to attend to. I had been planning for some time to make big changes to our Lake Placid home and wanted to take two weeks off in September to see the process launched. Terry had done the architecture work, and he was taking time off, too. We wanted to coordinate our schedules. Then when the year turned, I wanted to be sure that Marie and I could take our treasured skiing trip to Zürs and whatever cities in Europe had Bache offices that needed attention. As I wrote John in that September 15 memo, "I hope to be able to take my European vacation in March as perhaps I will not be able to go in 1977."

The timetable played out as I envisioned. I was elected CEO of Bache Halsey Stuart at the annual stockholders' meeting on November 23, 1976, and also of the Bache Group, the parent company. I retained the title of president as well. John, who was then 66, stayed on as chairman.

PHOTO GALLERY

Here I am at Lake Placid around 1928. It looks like I was cut out to be a sailor.

Striking a pose during my Primary Flight Training, Pine Bluff, Arkansas, January, 1943.

I earned my wings that summer, and Marie pinned them on. Pampa Army Air Field, Pampa, Texas, July 29, 1943.

Terry and Nancy as infants, in our apartment in Forest Hills, Queens, after the war. Things were crowded in those days.

A young Wall Streeter on the rise.

My brother Bob and me with our mother, Elsie Wolf Jacobs, at Lake Placid around 1955.

Zürs, Austria, was our winter family playground. Marie and I started ski trips with the kids in 1958 and we went every winter for over thirty years.

I cut quite a figure on the slopes (but Marie was a better skier)

Nancy grew up and married a great guy named Woof Haneman. This is them in their back yard in Rye, NY, with Patricia, on the left, and Nicolle, around 1986.

Marie and I defied the power boats and canoed to a party on Buck Island at Lake Placid, approx. 1985.

We got to be great friends with Annie and John Glenn, and I'm still close with the Glenns. This shot is from John's 1984 presidential campaign when I flew them from Naples to Cape Cod. L to R: Harry, Annie, Marie, John.

Marie and I attended Clark Clifford's eightieth birthday party at the Metropolitan Club, New York City, 1986. Clark was a good friend.

I was lucky enough to meet Joannie Patterson after Marie died. My minister and good friend David Harkness from the Irvington Presbyterian Church administered our vows in April, 1997. Her son Ruff, looking on, was our best man.

This is me and Joannie in front of King Air 150 YA around 1997, the year we were married.

Here I am sitting left seat, wearing my lucky flying sport jacket.

This shot is at historic Wings Field near Philadelphia. It's Terry's wife Sally Harrison, Terry, their sons (my grandsons) Steven and Andrew, and Joannie. We were the first plane in after they lengthened the runway, and they put us on TV.

These are my granddaughters, Patricia Haneman Cox and Nicolle Haneman Keally on Nicolle's wedding day, June 28, 2006, at Lake Placid. I'm at the helm of my 1958 Chris Craft, "White Cloud."

Terry's family is grown up now, too. Here are the four of them together: Andrew, Sally, Terry and Steven.

Andrew and Steven posing at the Benin-Togo border in West Africa. Andrew was a Peace Corps volunteer in Togo from 2007 to 2009.

Four generations on Christmas Eve, 2009: Chappy Cox; Patricia Haneman Cox; Breck Cox; Alex Keally; Hadley Keally; Nicolle Haneman Keally; me; and Nancy at Nancy's home in Rye.

Challenges

My first act as CEO was to call for an earlier opening of the New York Stock Exchange. I was no longer on the NYSE board. Terms of the governors, now called directors, were three years and I had come off the board in 1972. But I had continued to advocate for a longer trading day. Indeed, two years earlier in 1974, Bache and I had led the charge toward the four p.m. closing time that went into effect that year. Now it was time, I said in my speech to Bache stockholders after they elected me, for the exchange to open for trading at nine-thirty instead of ten in the morning. Along with the greater efficiency of a longer day, I said an earlier opening would give European investors more time to weigh their decisions on NYSE trades.

I saw my first job as CEO as risk aversion. The traders didn't like it, but I had had an adversarial relationship with them from the time in the early 60s when I started to spread my wings beyond syndicate manager. As CEO, I devoted the beginning of each day to looking over all the trading positions and making sure that nobody in the trading areas had excessive inventory – too many bonds or too many stocks or up near their limit. I kept a tight lid on credit lines. Our leverage was ten or twelve to one. A lot of our leverage came from financing margin accounts, which was a low risk business. But the positions in the corporate bond trading, government bond trading, arbitrage, all that was high risk. I watched all that like a hawk, and violent market downturns never really hurt us.

We had a rule that would sound insane today. Any trader who had a loss of $25,000 or more had to give me a memo explaining it within twenty-four hours. Major offenders never got a second chance.

The firm was in good shape at that point. We had quadrupled our earnings per share from 2 cents to 8 cents in the quarter ended October 31. Profits were up over 300 percent from a year earlier on a gain in revenues of 19.1 percent. The view from the top was rosy. And my fears about missing my European vacation in 1977 went unrealized. Marie and I went to Zürs and had our usual wonderful time.

That June, we improved our position in brokerage and investment banking and international arbitrage with a merger. Our partner was Shields Model Roland, a private firm with a handful of shareholders but a strong capital position. Shields and Model Roland, two similar firms, had only recently merged themselves within the past three years.

The deal was technically an acquisition that cost $25.9 million to buy out the thirty-five Shields Model Roland stockholders, but it felt like a merger. H. Virgil Sherrill was the CEO. We were very different. He was a World War II war hero from Deep South Mississippi who had shot down seven Japanese planes, blew up a destroyer, and received the Navy Cross. His sport was golf, and he was good at it -- he once won the Bing Crosby Pro-Am tournament at Pebble Beach. He and his wife Betty, a successful decorator, were very social. They had houses in Southampton and Hobe Sound, Florida, and were fixtures on the charity circuit. People on Wall Street said it would never work out. But as different as we were, we thought alike. I remained CEO of the Bache Group and Bache Halsey

Stuart Shields, which was the name of the new firm. Virg, as I quickly learned to call him as we became fast friends and effective working partners, took on the president's duties.

With what Shields brought to the table, we now had a $157 million capital base, 7,000 employees, and 168 offices in the U.S., Canada, throughout Europe, and in Hong Kong, Tokyo, and Singapore.

The deal was "truly a blockbuster," according to *The New York Times* in a story published that October. But the story was headlined: "Harry Jacobs: Woes Aplenty." It focused on the costs of operating our all-purpose headquarters on Gold Street, which we had designed for more sales people and data processors than we had ever needed given the softness in the stock market. "Our back end became too big for our front," I said. That meant one of my prime challenges was finding more acquisitions if I could, and extending our reach further into institutional markets.

One result of the merger was Frank Digaetano's resignation, early in 1978, as the Bache Group's vice chairman, treasurer and chief financial officer. The business press reported the resignation and speculated that he saw his path to the top blocked by the addition of Shields officers to the executive mix at the merged firm. We were also putting a lot of pressure on him to reduce operational costs, but it wasn't happening. Digaetano had been a great operations man, but I wasn't that sorry to see him go.

Crisis: The Belzbergs

Marie and I had finished the skiing part of our European vacation in March of 1979 and gone on to our traditional city visits. One stop was in Munich. I was in the Bache office there and happened to be looking at the stock ticker when I saw a big block of Bache stock – 60,000 shares -- go by. What's that? I thought. Was somebody making a play for Bache & Company?

When we got back I learned the buyer was Samuel Belzberg. Virg Sherrill had written me a memo back in January to say that Belzberg, "a very wealthy Canadian," owned about 300,000 shares of Bache stock. I learned that the Belzberg brothers – the others were Hyman and William – were well known in Canadian business circles. Their father Abraham had emigrated from Poland and the sons inherited his sharp eye for business. They were very acquisitive, but the most acquisitive was Sam, who operated out of Vancouver. Virg's memo also said that he "evidently has a somewhat varied reputation." I concluded very quickly that the Belzbergs were not our kind of people. I knew right away that they were trying to use

Bache as their route to respectability just like Sam Bronfman used Seagram's.

On one of my summers in Lake Placid when I was young, I came downstairs one day to find my mother and grandmother – she of the chauffeured Pierce Arrow – with their heads together in the corner. They were talking intensely about the news that Sam Bronfman, the bootlegger, had come to Lake Placid. Bronfman owned the Distillers Corporation based in Montreal. During Prohibition, he used to haul whiskey down from Canada to Malone, New York, just across the border, and then Dutch Schultz would pick it up and take it down to the thirsty speakeasies of New York City. Bronfman had a terrible reputation, but he bought Seagram's and decided he was going to change his reputation. So the first thing he did was take a cottage at the Whiteface Inn, an old resort at Lake Placid. My mother and grandmother disapproved. So did much of Lake Placid.

The next thing he did was hire Alfred Rose of the Proskauer Rose law firm as the attorney for Seagram's. Alfred Rose had a place on Moose Island in Lake Placid. The next thing he did after that was to have his daughter Phyllis, who was an architect, go to work for Kahn and Jacobs, my brother's firm. And later he had his son Edgar marry Ann Loeb, the daughter of John Loeb, the scion of Loeb Rhoades, one of the investment banking houses. So in fifteen or twenty years people forgot his reputation and he passed.

It turned out that Sam Belzberg had been accumulating our stock for some time, much of it purchased by Oppenheimer & Company in New York where his son worked. Nobody would say anything for the record except that he thought the stock was undervalued and was a good investment. But it was clear where he was going. I told Virg, "They're going to try and use me as the conduit to make themselves another Sam Bronfman. But they're going to do it over my dead body."

I wrote a memo to the files on April 5. It laid out my concerns in outline form for clarity as Josephine Mayer had taught me so many years before at Lincoln School:

1. It's a death fight.
2. The pattern is clear.
   a. They buy 40% to 50% of a company.
   b. They gain control and let other stockholders flop in complete disregard of their rights.

"Based on appraisal to date, the entry of Belzberg would cause tremendous damage to our firm and would be absolutely inimical to quality and character of Bache," I wrote under point number 5.

The rest of the memo suggested defensive measures. I wanted someone who knew the ins and outs of Washington to be involved. To me this meant Clark Clifford. If we could make a good case that the rights of stockholders were threatened, I thought we might be able to spur congressional hearings on the Belzbergs' interest. We certainly needed to retain a top-flight public relations firm, Ruder & Finn in this case, to work with our in-house department. We also needed to establish contact with outside investment bankers, and perhaps retain a Canadian law firm that could launch an investigation of the Belzbergs through its local resources.

By the start of the following week I had a memo in hand that recounted a meeting with Hyman Belzberg in Calgary, Alberta, where he ran the furniture business started by his father. The bottom line of the report was that Sam Belzberg wanted a seat on the Bache board "if they will have him."

We continued to accumulate information on Sam Belzberg and his intentions. One report, dated in May, said he would be a "gadfly" who would be letting Bache know about matters that displeased him. Virg Sherrill met with him and talked with him on the phone while I worked furiously behind the scenes. Their discussions were polite but inconclusive.

By July, Belzberg owned stock amounting to over 7.8 percent of Bache. We were signaling loud and strong that we didn't want him buying any more, and that we wouldn't have him on the board. We knew he was getting the message. But green-mailers hear that all the time, and it never stops them.

Through that summer, our relations with Belzberg were distant but cordial. At a meeting in September, 1979, the gloves came off.

Virg and I went to see Sam Belzberg in his suite at the Regency. The meeting lasted fifteen minutes, including the three calls he took to discuss real estate deals. He told us he was going to buy up 20 to 25 percent of our stock either on the open market or through a tender offer. Whether it was done amicably or not was up to us but we should let him know.

He grew more and more angry, apparently at our intention to rebuff him. His elbows were on the table and he slammed his right hand down repeatedly. His face got so purple and contorted with rage I thought he would have a stroke. Afterward, I wrote in a note for the file, "THIS WAS THE WORST BUSINESS MEETING I HAVE EVER HAD."

With the battle lines drawn, I met with the four outside directors (of the twelve-member board). I told them it was up to them if Belzberg got on the board, but if he did they were going to see my shoes crossing the threshold going out. I told them I thought it would be bad for the company if Belzberg had his way, and they agreed. On September 21, the board took the position that further Belzerg acquisitions were against the company's best interests.

I wrote Belzberg that following Monday. "The Board of Directors agree," I wrote, "that an increase in ownership by you of Bache shares would be contrary to the interests of Bache and its shareholders."

That November, I engineered a bylaw change that increased from 50 percent to 75 percent the percentage of ownership required to take over management control. Nevertheless, Belzberg persisted.

Crisis No. 2: The Hunts and Their Silver

Another set of brothers brought on our next crisis. This time it was the Hunt brothers of Dallas. Nelson Bunker Hunt and William Herbert Hunt were the sons of the famous Texas oilman, H. L. Hunt. They were big customers of Bache, dealing with our commodities department in agricultural products. During the 1970s, when inflation was such a threat that Nixon had imposed wage and price controls, they started buying silver as a hedge. Then in the late 1970s, they got together with some Saudis and allegedly tried to corner the world's silver market. By early 1980, they had about half the world supply.

All this buying forced the price of silver to unheard-of heights. It had been $5 an ounce early in 1979. In early 1980 it got to over $50 an ounce before it started falling. And when it started falling, it fell fast. At the same time, COMEX, the commodities exchange, tightened margin requirements. We were loaning the Hunts money to buy silver just like everybody else on Wall Street, but we were probably loaning them the most since we were handling their transactions. The Hunts sold to meet their margin calls, and the selling drove the price of silver lower.

Marie and I made our usual trip to Austria that March. One night not long after we arrived the phone rang in our room. It was John Curran, Bache's general counsel. "The Hunts didn't meet their margin call," he said.

Sweat started trickling down my chest and I said to Marie, "We're going home."

"We just got here," she said.

"You stay," I told her. "But I've got to go home."

We had a harrowing two weeks. Silver kept sliding. All the big Wall Street firms were in trouble, but we were in deepest. If silver went to under $10 I didn't know if we would be able to survive. The commodities area of Bache was a big department that Harold Bache had known a lot about and had helped to build up, but in all my training and years there I hadn't learned a lot about it. That was one area of the business where I was relatively ignorant – margin calls and all that. If I had had better training and education in commodities maybe we wouldn't have given the Hunts such a large line of credit.

Then the price of silver dropped by half – from $21.62 to $10.80 – in one day, March 27. I called an emergency meeting with the lawyers to decide how to handle the Hunts' accounts. All of a sudden I had an inspiration. I stood up and said, "I'm going to call Paul Volcker." Volcker had been appointed chairman of the Federal Reserve the year before by President Jimmy Carter.

Nobody but me thought it was a good idea, but I made the call. Of course, I didn't get him on the phone right away, but I told the secretary, "I want to speak to Chairman Volcker about a crisis of monumental proportions." He called me back pretty fast.

I told him about our exposure to the silver crisis and that we were going to be ruined if prices didn't stabilize. I ticked off the other firms that were in almost as deep as we were, including Merrill Lynch and the First National Bank of Chicago.

What I got from the conversation was that Volcker had no interest in seeing the price drop further, since that would be deflationary.

I don't know what he did, if anything, or even what he could have done, but we had a little quote machine set up in the meeting room and I had it set to display the silver quote. I don't remember if it was that day or the next day that silver got to $10 and stayed there. It just kept clicking $10, $10, $10.

And with that, the silver crisis abated, at least for Bache. But not the Hunts. They had so many silver contracts on the books, and they had had to put up margin every day, and if they didn't then we sold their contracts. We sold them out. The Saudis reportedly lost money, but the Hunts were ruined. This was too bad since they had bought about $5 million of our shares to help fend off the Belzbergs. That stock represented 6.6 percent of the company. The shares were now in limbo while they tried to bail themselves out. But I never saw them again after that.

The Belzberg Fight Escalates

Bache stock didn't suffer in the long run from the silver crisis. By July the Belzberg interests had bought another chunk of shares and brought their ownership up to 8.2 percent. Every time somebody asked him about it, as more and more of the business press was doing, Sam Belzberg said he thought it was a good investment at a price of around $13. Soon afterward, gobbling up another 115,000 shares, they owned 10.2 percent of Bache.

I met briefly with him in July with none of the previous histrionics, and he sent me a cordial note afterwards inviting me to Vancouver where he kept his headquarters. "It would be nice for us to get to know each other a little better," he wrote. That was something I had no intention of doing.

Around that same time some private investigations we had launched into the Belzbergs began to pay off. It wasn't long before Delayne Gold, the woman in charge of our public relations operation, took a ride on the Staten Island ferry with a reporter from the *Wall Street Journal*. Soon unflattering episodes from the Belzbergs' history were in the news.

Late in October the Belzbergs demanded a meeting to know why we wouldn't put them on the board or do business with them. William and Sam Belzberg and one of their people met me, Virg, and John Curran over lunch in New York. Questions – and suspicions – flew back and forth in the guise of strained small talk. The suspicion was justified on our part. We had learned just that morning that they had bought another big chunk of Bache shares. These were from the Hunt brothers, part of the stake they had purchased early in the year.

Our business plans came in for criticism. We had recently bought Albert Bender, an insurance brokerage that in turn had been buying smaller insurance brokers. They wanted to know why we were doing this, since the companies didn't add to our book value. We said we saw them as adding earning power. (Indeed, these companies combined would make Bache the eleventh largest property and casualty insurer in the United States.)

We told them that every time Bache employees heard that the Belzbergs had bought more Bache stock, there was a loss of morale. They said they would like us to show the public that they did not have "horns."

The meeting ended as the others had, with Sam Belzberg vowing that the Belzberg interests would buy more Bache shares, and my repeating that they were never going to gain a position on our board.

The Hunt stock, on which the Hunts made around $6 a share, gave the Belzbergs 11.2 percent of Bache. They told the *Wall Street Journal* they were going for "at least 15 percent." Our position was getting more desperate. Then Sam Belzberg informed us he was attending our annual meeting at the end of November. He came, asked annoying questions, and then kept demanding to see me alone, first in my office, then in Toronto. My conclusion, in a memo I wrote for the files: "There is no doubt that they are substantially building up the pressure on us and especially me. They are putting a 'gun to our head' to get on the Board."

Sam Belzberg and I met alone in the middle of December. We met at a conference room at the American Airlines Admirals Club at LaGuardia Airport. I scribbled a memo in the car on my way home. "The meeting started off very cordially," I wrote. But "as the meeting wore on, the cordiality dimmed and the insistence on 1 – 2 seats on the board grew."

He kept saying, "I will bring a lot to the party." He wanted to know by January 7 or 8 if he was to get a seat on the board. If not, he was going to "make a move." He talked about assembling 40 to 45 percent of the shares and taking over management.

It was at some point during this meeting that Belzberg made a declaration that I found preposterous. He said, "You don't like me because I'm Jewish."

"That's not true," I said. "I just don't like you."

During the Christmas season and into the New Year, we heard rumor after rumor that the Belzbergs were soliciting Bache stock in blocks of at least 50,000 shares. By January 1981 I saw one last chance to pull a rabbit out of the hat. I asked Clark Clifford if he would mediate with Sam Belzberg. He said he would. I told Belzberg that a famous American diplomat might be able to help arbitrate our way out of this disagreeable situation. He agreed to meet Clark in Washington.

They met at a waiting room at Washington National Airport, in a waiting room because Belzberg was afraid of being taped. Clark's message was this: "Mr. Belzberg, the directors of Bache and Company have authorized me to tell you that you or your family can never be on the board of Bache."

With that, Belzberg went ape and started buying more and more of our stock. Late in January, the Belzbergs owned almost 17 percent of the outstanding shares. Nevertheless, at my urging the nominating committee of the board rejected his request for one or two board seats. By February, he had almost 20 percent of our shares.

In the meantime, I was lobbying Ron Stafford, the New York State senator from the North Country that included Lake

Placid, to introduce a law requiring anybody who owned 25 percent of a stock broker-dealer with offices in New York State to be approved by the attorney general. The legislation moved quickly.

I woke up one morning around the first of March, 1981, and read that the Belzbergs had gotten their stake up to 22 percent. It was clear to me then that we could not go on. I had fought the fight of my life and kept the Belzbergs off the board, but now we needed help. We had used First Boston as our advisor, and I called up George Shinn, the CEO. "We can't hang on any longer," I told him. "We need to find a buyer."

Within two weeks he came back with an offer from Prudential. And we sold to them. The deal was announced on March 18. Two weeks later, it seemed as if we had started a trend. American Express announced it was buying Shearson Loeb Rhodes and adding investment and stock trading services to its business array. Then Dean Witter sold to Sears and Salomon to Phillips Brothers.

I was exhausted at the end of the long fight. Even Marie had suffered an unexpected side effect. She developed an irregular heartbeat and couldn't exercise for six months. Since she was a natural and enthusiastic athlete, this irritated her to no end.

Pru-Bache

I was a little surprised that Prudential was lurking out there as a buyer. But it made sense. Prudential was selling life and car insurance to customers that numbered in the millions. To offer those customers additional financial services such as stock trades and mutual fund accounts put them one up on banks, which were prohibited from buying or becoming retail stockbrokers under laws enacted back in the Great Depression. It also gave Prudential greater control of its own huge investment portfolio.

Once George Shinn and First Boston put us together, Virg and I hammered out the outlines of the deal with Prudential's vice chairman and chief financial officer Frank Hoenemeyer over about ten days. The deal I presented to the Bache Group board was straightforward -- $385 million in cash. Although Prudential was a mutual company, meaning nobody could get Pru's shares for their interest and we'd have to pay capital gains taxes (then 29 percent), there was never any doubt that the board would approve the sale. Nobody wanted to end up in the Belzbergs' hands.

It was a good deal for everyone who owned Bache stock, the Belzbergs included. The purchase price of $32 a share gave them a $29 million profit. At that they came out better than I did. The public offering back in 1971 had diluted my ownership to a little over 1 percent (Virg Sherrill owned 1.74 percent) but I took away a little over $4 million before taxes from the sale.

Another part of the deal was that Bache management would remain in place. I stayed on as CEO of what was now the Bache arm of Prudential (renamed Prudential-Bache Securities) and Virg stayed on as president. That lasted for a year. Then the ax fell.

On July 16, 1982, Dave Sherwood, the president of the Prudential, came to see me and Virg. He told us they had hired George Ball, the president of E. F. Hutton, as the new CEO of Prudential-Bache. I was crushed, totally crushed, to say nothing of surprised. In retrospect I should not have been.

I stayed on as chairman in charge of risk management. Virg oversaw investment banking. After three years, in 1985, I left the boardroom and the main Pru-Bache office, which Ball had moved from Gold Street to a new building near the South Street Seaport, back to Gold Street where we still had our back office and a few branch office operations. There I started an investment advisory boutique with Saul Eisenberg, my colleague of some forty years. He's a sound and good manager and an all-around quality person. We were still under the umbrella of Prudential-Bache Securities and we had an uninspiring but accurate name. We were the Investment Supervisory Group. It was very much like the department I had worked in when I joined Bache in 1946.

The department was just the two of us and a small staff. We had about 150 clients whom we charged a small fee to manage their investments, and we built the assets up to about $350 million. All the clients were individuals except for the Teamsters Union, and I recused myself from work on their account. The work was very enjoyable, profitable, and intellectually stimulating. After my long climb up the corporate ladder, I was out of management completely. I didn't miss it much.

I didn't miss it, but I thought I had made some major contributions during my time at the firm. Number one was the retailing of good mutual funds to small investors. Bache's entry into the institutional and trading business was another thing I brought to the table. I helped Bache get started in investment banking, although we never had more than a small staff of ten or twelve. Our acquisition of Halsey Stuart, the banking firm, gave us a big leg up in that department. John Leslie and I did that together. And our acquisition of Stein Brothers & Boyce, an old Baltimore firm from the 1850s and half a dozen other regional firms including Shields, which brought Virg on board, happened on my watch. Our problem was that our back end was too big for our front, so we had to build the sales force and mergers were part of that.

In light of the events of 2008 into 2009, perhaps the very best thing I did was to keep a firm hand on all of the firm's positions in stocks and bonds. Any trader who strayed from the proper path was quickly fired.

Equally important, I kept strong control on our capital ratio. A few years after we went public, we came back to the market for a $45 million bond issue with warrants. We didn't need the money and it diluted the stocks, but I was intent on maintaining a strong capital foundation.

Poor investing control, too much leverage, and just all around terrible judgment is what sank the firms that went under in the recent crisis. Seasoned Wall Streeters forgot lessons they should have learned at the start of their careers, and got dumb, stupid and greedy. That would never have happened to Bache on my watch!

We never did huge mergers like Sandy Weill. I was afraid of the operational problems. But he did it brilliantly, starting as Carter, Berlind, Potoma & Weill and growing it into what became Citicorp and later Citigroup. Of course, in the spring of 2009 in the middle of what was being called the worst financial crisis since the Great Depression, Citigroup stock was selling for under a dollar. More about that later.

Culture Clash

The day after the Pru deal closed in early June, Prudential CEO Bob Beck invited Virg and me over to a big meeting in the boardroom at Pru's headquarters in Newark. We walked in and saw maybe forty executives all sitting around a great big table. Bob opened the meeting with the words, "Good morning, people."

"Good morning, Bob," they responded in perfect unison.

I felt like I'd walked into a grade school classroom at the start of the school day. Bache's Midwestern branch managers were a far more sophisticated bunch. I pictured what they would have done if I had opened a meeting with a greeting like that. They would have pelted me with eggs and rotten tomatoes and hooted me out of the room. The change in cultures was unbelievable.

I figured out one reason for it. That enormous company, with well over a hundred thousand employees, was a mutual company. None of the people who worked there could share in its ownership. It was a company full of employees but no owners. I think ownership makes people work harder in most cases. That's one of the things that made everything so different.

If one culture had understood and appreciated the other and vice versa things might have gone better. But the chemistry between them was just not possible. This was true throughout Wall Street. In almost every case where an insurance company or a bank bought a securities firm, the merger ended up catastrophically. In our case, the Prudential wanted to project a budget three years ahead of time. A securities firm could certainly budget its expenses, but nobody could budget future revenues and profits. It's like predicting the future. It's just not there.

Different personality types defined the culture gap as well. A typical Prudential executive would probably have emerged from a blue-collar family, gone to a Midwestern school like the University of Michigan and then, if he or she was very bright, gone on to an Eastern business school. That's different from Wall Streeters. They would have gone to an Ivy League school and a business school, or they would have been tops in mathematics at a New York public school and never gone to college but ended up as a firm's head trader. They were just different kinds of people. You could find lots of people on Wall Street who never went to college. Nobody like that would ever get inside the Prudential.

Talking to reporters after the deal closed, I had made optimistic predictions about the outcome of the sale. My forecasts turned out to be right in only one respect. The stockholders did get fair value for the stock. But otherwise my forecast was totally lousy.

I had said the deal would be good for Bache's customers because they would have the capital of The Prudential behind them. That was true for a time, but Prudential failed to make an impact in the investment banking business and eventually sold what was left of the Bache component to Wachovia. So that was not a good forecast. I said the employees would be better off because they would have a more stable owner, one immune from the kinds of attacks the Belzbergs represented. That turned out to be totally false because once they combined the operations everybody got fired except for the sales people.

And George Ball turned out to be an example of misplaced ambition. He had been running Pru-Bache for two or three years when the E. F. Hutton scandal broke. The company pleaded guilty to 2,200 counts of mail and wire fraud. They had been spreading bank deposits all over the country and then writing checks on these banks for larger amounts than the deposits. Then they used the difference – the float – to reduce their own bank loans. This, in effect, was money laundering made possible by check kiting. No individuals were charged, but that was the end of E. F. Hutton.

What happened at Prudential-Bache was even worse. He got the company heavily involved in the sale of tax shelters. But the brokers selling these "investment partnerships" didn't disclose their risk. The Securities and Exchange Commission eventually got involved, and ordered Pru-Bache to pay $2 billion in penalties and restitution to make their customers whole. It was the largest settlement in Wall Street history at the time.

We never got involved in tax shelters much on my watch. I didn't like them because I didn't understand them, and I still don't. And I never lost that feeling that Lawrence Bache Rossbach had drummed into me early on, that handling people's money was a sacred trust, not an opportunity to fleece them. I believe Bache had a long legacy of doing the right thing, from Leopold Kann, Jules Bache's uncle who founded the firm, to Jules Bache to Harold Bache to John Leslie to me. We believed that the customer came first and that prudence outweighed risk.

By the time the tax shelter scandal broke, the firm was losing money, and after several years of losses George Ball resigned in 1991.

Wick Simmons replaced Ball as CEO, and he proved to be a distinguished and effective chairman. Wick was born to the purple. He was a young executive at Hayden Stone, where his great-grandfather had been one of the founders, when it was taken over by Sandy Weill. On his watch at Pru-Bache, he contemplated merging the firm with Donaldson, Lufkin & Jenrette (DLJ), which would have been a splendid opportunity. But The Prudential would not back him up, and he went on to chair the NASDAQ. He consulted with me often. Our friendship continues to this day and as I write this I look forward to attending the 2009 U.S. Open tennis matches at Flushing as his guest.

Outside Interests

The day after Dave Sherwood told me I was going to be replaced as CEO, I went to see Clark Clifford. We had grown close over the years. I turned to him often for advice, and I always found his advice to be great.

I told Clark what had happened, and asked how he thought I should respond. He said, "Well, you're still chairman. You should take that title and run with it. Use the next three years to your advantage. Do other things outside the company. Get to know some other people. Do some pro bono work."

He was right on target, as usual. I did what he said, and I did it with a vengeance. The National Defense University at Ft. McNair in Washington is a grad school for top level military and national security officials. It looks at a wide range of national and international matters and does research and strategic studies. In other words, it is a military and security think tank with components of diplomacy, politics, and economics. It operates on public money, but the National Defense University Foundation supplements the public budget by raising private funds to help the NDU fulfill its mission.

I connected with the NDU through my friend Henry Clay Hofheimer , a distinguished citizen of Norfolk, Virginia, who knew a lot of senior naval personnel connected to the U.S. Navy base there. He had gotten involved with the NDU through them, and he asked me at some point if I wanted to serve on the board. I said yes, and found it really interesting rubbing shoulders with a group of top military people. It was totally different from anything I'd done before. This was in 1983 or 1984 and later I became board chairman. I not only enjoyed the work and the people very much, I was overwhelmingly impressed with their abilities.

I became a director of the Center for National Policy, which is a Democratic think tank. I became chairman of the board of Paul Smith's College near Lake Placid. I became a trustee of the Trudeau Institute, which is a descendant of the Trudeau Sanitarium at Saranac Lake near Lake Placid and was founded by Dr. Frank Trudeau, the father of Garry Trudeau of "Doonesbury" fame. Frank was my dear friend for many years. True to its origins, the Trudeau Institute does basic research in tuberculosis and allied diseases. On the corporate side, I served on the boards of many Prudential-Bache mutual funds, which honed my investment expertise.

But my most important outside interest was the national Democratic Business Council. The council was formed in 1980 by the Democratic National Committee to give Democrats a conduit for donations from business people. It was an area where Republicans had traditionally had a massive advantage, to the frustration of progressive business leaders. An individual membership cost $10,000, a corporate membership $15,000. I got deeply involved from 1982 on. It was time-consuming, but I loved it even though Marie, who was at my side for almost everything, didn't care much for politics. A few years later I became the council's chairman. In this role I planned events, helped to raise money for Democratic candidates and the party, and met regularly with its top movers and shakers.

After Bill Clinton became president, these contacts produced an offer I had coveted for a long time. From the beginning of my long love affair with Austria that started with our first trip to Zürs in 1958, I had imagined myself as U.S. ambassador there and made no secret of the fact. In March 1993, about two months after Clinton was inaugurated, I was in my office with Lang Stevenson, a client who had been the treasurer of Bache, and Saul Eisenberg when Dick Schmidt called. He had worked with Vice President Walter Mondale during the Carter years and recruited personnel for various Democratic administrations. He asked me if I was still interested in being ambassador to Austria.

It pained me but I said no. I had undergone surgery for prostate cancer the previous July at Memorial Sloan Kettering and it was not successful. In the aftermath, I was getting injections of Lupron once a month and taking six Flutamide pills daily. Both are hormone manipulators and the Flutamide especially was knocking me for a loop both emotionally and physically. I didn't think I could perform the way an American ambassador is expected to perform, even in a friendly country like Austria.

Time passed me by on that one. A year later my oncologist discontinued the Flutamide, which straightened me out medically. A year after that, I met my second great love. That wouldn't have happened if I had taken the ambassadorial appointment, so life evens things out.

John and Annie Glenn

John Glenn was prominent in the Democratic Party when I headed the Business Council. I hadn't known John when he was first elected to the Senate from Ohio in 1974. I knew his reputation, of course. You almost couldn't be an American and not know about John Glenn, the World War II and Korean War fighter pilot who was one of the seven original Mercury Astronauts and the first American to orbit the Earth in 1962 at the height of the Cold War space race between the United States and the Soviet Union. It was that flight – three times around the globe in a spacecraft he named Friendship 7 – that cemented John in the pantheon of heroes. The flight was broadcast live on TV and radio. People stood in front of department store TV displays listening to the talk between John and Mission Control. But when the capsule was re-entering the atmosphere, John's voice went out and there was only static. There was only one explanation – the spacecraft had burned up on re-entry. The whole nation held its breath and a lot of people prayed. I was one of them. Then John's voice came on again and the whole country was relieved. John was oblivious to the whole thing and was cool as a cucumber when the Navy picked him up after Friendship 7 splashed down out in the Atlantic.

So in 1978 or 1979, when my friend, Bob Davis from Columbus, Ohio, asked me if I wanted to fly right seat on a trip from Westchester County to Washington to meet John Glenn, I jumped at the chance.

We met in John's Senate office. I don't remember what the meeting was about, except that it was somewhat perfunctory. But John took note that I had flown during World War II, albeit not overseas in combat. After a gap of about fifteen years when money was tight, I had resumed flying in 1965, renewed my commercial pilot's license, and graduated from a single-engine Cessna with fixed landing gear to a twin-engine Aero Commander and then a pressurized King Air B-100. I rented the planes I flew, but John owned his own twin-engine Beechcraft Baron, so we had flying in common. A few months later, somebody called from John's office to say that he and Annie were coming to New York. Could Marie and I join them for dinner?

We met at the famous 21 Club on West 52nd Street. Ed Fergus, our governmental affairs guy at Bache, was along. That night was the beginning of a friendship. Marie and Annie got along famously. They were very much alike, two small-town girls who were completely unfazed by fame and all that stuff. Annie didn't exist in John's shadow. She had a track record of her own after she conquered her profound stuttering problem. John and I got along famously, too. I think we closed 21 that night.

After that we started to see them more and more. Then John started sending out feelers, trying to decide if he should seek the 1984 Democratic presidential nomination. The first discussions were held in the fall of 1982. I jumped on the bandwagon.

The Democratic field was wide-open leading up to 1984. Senator Ted Kennedy decided not to seek the nomination, and that left Walter Mondale, Gary Hart, and John among the big names in the field. John announced in April 1983, in his hometown of New Concord, Ohio. It was a memorable occasion combining pageantry, patriotism, and great promise. The race was on.

We had the time of our lives in that campaign. Marie and I gave a big and very successful fundraiser for John at the University Club in New York. We traveled to events with them, and I flew them around on a couple of trips, using a pilot not because I didn't trust myself but because I wanted the extra margin of safety for someone who might be our next president. I flew him from Columbus, Ohio, to Lebanon, New Hampshire, when he was speaking at Dartmouth, and from Pittsburgh to Washington, D.C. after a fundraiser in Pittsburgh. John was disturbed by always having to raise money, but we had a good time on those trips.

The campaign ultimately came a cropper. John dropped out after the "Super Tuesday" primaries in March 1984.

At that point I shifted gears and helped John raise money to retire his campaign debt. It was around $3 million, which seems like hardly anything in light of today's non-stop campaigns. The important thing is that our friendship with John and Annie survived after the campaign and they're my friends to this day. We've always been there for each other. I was blind trustee for half of his investments for the latter part of his days in the Senate, and they took care of me after the two great losses of my life. I've been out to Ohio for several events involving them, including Annie's honorary degree from Ohio State where she gave a great speech, and John's address to the 2009 graduating class at Ohio State. We talk or write at least once a week about things in general.

Marie

Marie and I rarely disagreed on things. The one thing we had argued about, though, was her smoking. I had occasionally smoked cigars and a pipe, but not recently, and never cigarettes. She was a cigarette smoker when I met her and kept it up despite my objections until we moved to Irvington in the fall of 1969. When we got there I saw a Smoke Enders course advertised at the nearby Hilton Hotel. I told her I was signing up for it because I wanted to see what it was like and if it would help me help her quit. She reluctantly said if I was going to spend that much time and money she would do it, too.

She took the eight-week course and at the end of it, she quit.

For almost twenty years after that it was easy to forget that she had ever smoked. We returned to Zürs in 1988 as usual. It was our thirty-second trip. I was 66 years old and my corporate duties were largely behind me, except for the lovely trips Marie and I made several times each year to the meetings of the Pru-Bache mutual fund boards. There were also the First Australia Funds board trips to more exotic destinations – London and

Paris in June and Hong Kong and Sydney in December. Saul Eisenberg and I still ran our small and successful investment advisory boutique under the Pru-Bache umbrella. But other than that it was skiing and playing tennis, enjoying our family and Lake Placid and the life we had built together.

Every time we had skied, Marie had gone first. She was a strong, natural athlete, a better skier in the tough places and a better skier all around. She took the steepest slopes fearlessly. I was a little chicken of heights and the runs at Zürs were sometimes almost vertical, at least it seemed that way to me. Even at home, in the fall when the leaves fell and it was time to clean the gutters, Marie got up on the roof while I held the ladder for her.

But as we neared the end of our trip to Zürs that year, I sensed something was wrong. She went up for a last run one day. I stayed at the bottom of the mountain and watched her coming down, and she looked very frail.

When we left Zürs we went to St. Moritz to meet some friends from Lake Placid for a little bit more skiing. Our dear friend and ski instructor Willi Böckle went with us. The last day when we came off the mountain Marie burst into tears and hugged Willi for dear life. I think she, too, sensed something bad was coming.

But life went on. Early that fall, we went up to Lake Placid where we had always enjoyed canoeing and hiking together. We had spent hours on end just the two of us paddling along the lake shore and enjoying the spectacular scenery that never grew old. On October 1, a Saturday, we hiked to Rainbow Falls, a beautiful waterfall that is one of the highest in the Adirondacks. We had done it many times before. It was a spot we always loved. This time, though, once we took in the falls and hiked back to the trailhead where it was another fifteen minutes to the parking lot, Marie asked if I could get the car and bring it around while she waited. This was highly unusual. I left her sitting on a rock while I went to get the car. She looked exhausted.

We drove back to Irvington the next day. Marie had her regular medical checkup scheduled for that Tuesday.

I went down to the city that morning as usual. I had a driver named Dennis who was one of my remaining perks from Prudential-Bache. When he dropped me off at home that evening Marie was sitting on the patio looking out across the Hudson River with a faraway look on her face. When I came out she looked at me and said, "I have to go for a CAT scan at White Plains Hospital tomorrow."

A chill went through me. I knew instantly that she had lung cancer and I sat down with her and took her hands in mine. I think she knew it, too. When that first shock subsided, determination took its place. "You're not going to White Plains Hospital," I said.

I called Virg Sherrill right away. He chaired the Board of Overseers of the Memorial Sloan Kettering Cancer Center in New York dating back to when I was CEO of Bache and he was president. Sloan Kettering was and is probably the top cancer treatment center in the country. I told him that Marie needed a CAT scan right away. He would have set it up for the next day but she had a theater matinee date with two friends she didn't want to break. She went in for the scan on Thursday.

The result was just what I had feared. The scan showed a spot the size of a fifty-cent piece on her right lung. The Sloan Kettering doctors also showed us, on the x-ray her internist had taken the year before, the shadowy area that should have prompted him to order a CAT scan at that time. I was furious. The cancer had been growing for at least a year unchecked and probably had already metastasized.

Marie put on a brave front. "Everything's going to be all right," she said while the doctors were scheduling more tests and an expedited surgery. I knew her bravery was for my benefit, because I was scared to death.

She was operated on within a week. She wrote me a letter from the hospital saying that we'd be back on the ski slopes very soon. Six weeks later she began a course of radiation therapy. It was hard on her, but she was right about the skiing. We did not return to Zürs in 1989, but that spring we skied in Lake Placid for six days. It was hard on her, though.

Still, we maintained a relatively normal life through that summer and into the next year. She took more radiation. We returned to Lake Placid that summer, 1990, and although she was weak we enjoyed ourselves amid the scenery and the visits of our friends and family.

We had a routine that we followed when we were ready to come home at the end of the summer. One part of Marie's routine was to make sure the dishes were washed and put away and ready for the next time. I did the chores that were my part of the routine and then saw the untouched dishes. I went to find her. She was upstairs sitting on the bed, oblivious to our departure. I knew the cancer had spread to her brain.

Back at Sloan Kettering, the surgeons operated for six and a half hours. After that, she began a course of devastating chemotherapy, first at Sloan Kettering. Dennis would drive us both to New York in the morning and home again later. It killed me to see the effect the chemo had on her. Her hair fell out. She was weak and nauseous. This went on through the spring of 1991. She fought like a tiger. I was so proud of her.

We celebrated my seventieth birthday at a party at the Hotel Carlyle in New York with many of our best and oldest friends – John and Annie Glenn, Clark and Marny Clifford, Virg and Betty Sherrill among them – and Marie held her own among the partygoers. Annie and John came up to the house the next day for a visit before Dennis drove them to the airport.

That was at the end of June. By the fourth of July, the doctors told us that further treatment would be useless. Marie's decline was fairly rapid after that. Mabel Drake and Shirley Brewster, household managers who had been with us for years, anchored a team of caregivers. Gretl Wutte, our former housekeeper whom we had brought over from Austria, came from Florida. Nancy and Terry and their families were selfless with their attention. They gave me strength.

Even with all of their support, I needed to process what was happening. I had met Karen Fagerstrom, John Glenn's daughter-in-law who was married to his son David, an M.D. Karen was a child psychologist, and she suggested that I write my feelings down. I was to dwell not on Marie's pending death, but on the great happiness we had shared for many years. This seemed like a good prescription, and I took it. In a long letter to Karen written on September 1, which fell on the Labor Day weekend, I described our special relationship:

"The main thing I think about is that Marie and I have been wrapped together into a tight little cocoon, and we have our kids and a large family and a very, very few special friends – but it's been especially Marie and me. I have always worshipped her. To me she was, and is, and always will be my heroine.

"To say that my marriage to Marie has been a marriage made in heaven is a severe understatement. She has been my total life for almost fifty years and everything that has happened to me that is good is only related to the support and love and warmth that she has given me and I cannot imagine how I can handle it without her."

There was much more. I told Karen I had written what I wanted to say. That night I kissed Marie goodnight and she was able to respond. That was a small blessing, but I still hurt all over.

Marie died at home early in the morning of September 8, 1991. We had been married forty-eight years, nine months and eight days.

When I look back on the almost three years of her illness, I feel such gratitude. Friends and family rallied around from the beginning. I remember the time not only for Marie's courage and endurance under the ravages of both the cancer and the therapy that she endured, but also for the warmth of the love and friendship we received, and that we could not have done without. Nancy in particular was a total tower of strength for Marie, and for me.

I was bereft after Marie died. As Virg Sherrill said in his eulogy, I was Marie's Harry, and she was Harry's Marie. But I had to laugh when he hit me with a couple of zingers. Marie would have liked that. The funeral was to celebrate her life, not cast a pall of gloom over those who had loved her and seen her life and spirit and her courage.

Virg referred to that courage. He recounted my calling him from Zürs on our vacations describing Marie's feats on the slopes and said, "I would say to myself, 'Marie's bravery on the slopes is nothing compared to her bravery in getting in that airplane with you at the controls.'"

With that remark, Virg put things in perspective. John Glenn also spoke eloquently at the funeral, which brought some 400 people to the Irvington Presbyterian Church. The other speaker was Tommy Rosenwald, my sister Kitty's son. It was too much for me and Nancy and Terry, but we were grateful to hear of the impact Marie had on others. At the end of the service there was no doubt, if indeed there ever had been, that Marie was loved, cherished, and admired, and that she liked to have fun. It was a tribute to a wonderful life.

My Brothers and Sisters

Deaths in the family are never easy. My mother had died in 1983 in her hundredth year, and it would have been a blessing if she had died earlier. Her last seven or eight years were just terrible. She was blind and lost her hearing and then her mind and she wouldn't have wanted that.

But her long life balanced my father's early death at 60. My brother Bob split the difference and then some. He inherited the family gene for architecture from our father. (It bypassed me but lodged in my son Terry.) Since Bob was sixteen years older we almost inhabited two different lifetimes, and as I said the age difference made him an occasional father substitute. I was still at Lincoln School when he lived in Paris and worked for Charles-Édouard Jeanneret-Gris, the famous architect and designer known as Le Corbusier. After that he helped steer my course into early adulthood and marriage.

Marriage was a field that Bob knew well. He was married four times. His first wife was Nan Cullman, whose brother Joseph F. Cullman III took their father's investment in a British company called Benson & Hedges and built it into the world-wide tobacco and corporate giant Philip Morris. That marriage lasted twenty-two years and produced three children. A much shorter marriage followed, to Ellen Dribben (who would go on to marry Rene Lafleur), and then an even shorter one that hardly bears mentioning. In 1966 he married Margot Helland. He was 61 and she was 27, but that was the one that would last.

He partnered with Ely Jacques Kahn in 1940 to form Kahn & Jacobs. The firm became a major player in commercial architecture in New York. It employed some two hundred architects and designed such iconic structures as the original American Airlines Terminal at Idlewild (now JFK) Airport with its enormous stained-glass façade. Bob was a terrific salesman as well as a top-flight architect, and as his commissions increased, he embraced trappings of the good life.

He was an enthusiastic outdoorsman who loved to hunt and fish. After he and Margot were married they went on wildlife and hunting safaris in Kenya, Tanzania, and Botswana. Bob didn't hang trophies on the wall but brought back animal skins that he had made into rugs.

He was just as avid about fishing. Through a close friend, Air Force General and Chief of Staff Tom White, he was asked to join a small group of top Air Force brass in a salmon fishing camp in Labrador. You had to fly to Goose Bay and then take a float plane another 150 miles into the wilderness. Bob asked me to join him there for fishing many times, but I never did. I didn't like fishing nearly as much as he did, maybe because he took me fishing so often when I was a little kid.

At some point in the 1950s he joined the Dutchess Valley Rod and Gun Club near Pawling, New York. He rented and later bought a house on the grounds where he spent many weekends. He and Margot kept horses there and rode the local trails. A trout stream ran behind the house where he fished and elsewhere the 500 acres the club owned were devoted to hunting ducks and pheasant. I enjoyed hunting now and then, and when Terry got old enough we often joined Bob for weekends hunting.

One weekend when Terry was fourteen we went up for a hunting weekend. We spent the morning shooting ducks and in the afternoon shifted to pheasant. Terry was at the top of a hill with his .410 shotgun and I was down in the dip between hills when the dogs flushed a big pheasant that took off with a loud flapping of wings. The bird flew low and Terry took aim, fired, and nearly hit me. I could feel the pellets ruffling over my red hunting cap. He rushed down to make sure I was okay. It was something neither of us would ever forget.

The real estate depression of the 1970s hit Bob's business hard. Ely Jacques Kahn died in 1972 and the firm survived for a couple more years before Bob sold out to a huge firm with projects all over the world. He didn't like working for somebody else, so at that point he essentially retired to Pawling.

His health went downhill in the 1980s. He had had a massive heart attack years earlier, but recovered to go on those grueling African safaris that required a great deal of walking. Around 1990 he developed Parkinson's disease, but it was a bad heart that killed him in November, 1993. Like Marie, he died at home. He was 88 years old. Margot was a great wife to Bob in his declining years. I still stay in close touch with her and watch her investments.

I admired Bob greatly. He had an amazing way with people, and they gravitated naturally to him. He was six-feet three-inches tall, was strikingly handsome, and had what Margot called a "roguish charm." We spoke on the phone almost every day, not just about his investments, which I handled with Saul for more than thirty years, but about architecture, the outdoors, and life. He also talked on the phone with Terry after he became an architect, and I suspect Bob might have enjoyed those conversations even more, an uncle and his nephew sharing a professional bond.

My sisters were cut from the same crazy quilt of cloth. Kitty, the older of the two, was attractive and sophisticated. She and her husband Ed Rosenwald returned to New York after their brief stint in Memphis, and lived on Park Avenue. They were madly in love with each other, and they both died too young, Ed in 1969 and Kitty in 1984. In addition to Tommy, they had two other sons: Peter, who was Tommy's twin, and Johnny, the oldest. All three went to Deerfield and Dartmouth and two had careers on Wall Street.

Jane, nine years older than me, married her husband Alexander Moffat late in life and lived long. But hers was not a happy life despite the years she was granted. She never had children; she was very self-centered and never found things to suit her. Despite that, I was in touch with her frequently and had lunch at her apartment at least twice a month. She died in 2006 at the age of 93 and at the end she was incapacitated like my mother, enduring several years of dementia and needing care around the clock.

Those are among the reasons I don't want to live too long.

Joannie

The best result of one of Bob's failed marriages was that it led me to my second wife. A couple of years after Marie died, I started flying cross-country with John MacLaren in King Air 150YA, which he managed for its owner. John was an accomplished pilot as well, and I trusted him whether I was flying left seat or right seat. I used these summer trips to keep my license current and also to keep up with a sprawling network of friends that dated back years.

I always stopped in Sun Valley, Idaho, to see Ellen Lafleur. Even though her marriage to Bob had been short and unpleasant, I had remained friends with Ellen and was very fond of her. I also liked her ski instructor husband Rene. I was never there very long but Ellen would always throw a dinner party for me and introduce me to an eligible widow or divorcee. The first of these was a woman I simply found weird. The second was the widow of the head of the Sun Valley Ski School. She was very nice but there were no sparks between us. The third was Joannie Patterson.

Just like with Marie, I fell in love with Joannie instantly. I sat next to her but we didn't get to talk much because of the party.

I had to leave at nine o'clock because we had to be wheels-up early the next morning on the flight to our next stop. I don't remember what it was. What I did know was that I had to see Joannie Patterson again as soon as possible.

This was the summer of 1995. When I got home in August, I looked ahead and saw that I had a mutual fund directors' meeting in Naples, Florida, that October. Those were always fun, with recreation, good meals, and lots of social time between the business sessions. I called Joannie and wrote her and asked if she would join me.

It turned out that she was going to be going through Florida at that time on her way to Puerto Rico, where her sister Barb and Barb's husband Jim Cimino, who ran a hugely successful food and wine distributorship out of Old San Juan, lived about half the time. So she said yes. Being of the old school, I booked separate hotel rooms.

She arrived on a late flight and showed up after dark during a torchlight dinner the directors were having on the beach. She didn't know a soul except me, and she didn't know me all that well, even if she had been able to find me in the dark. But she handled it well and blended in beautifully. Two days later she won the tennis tournament.

We flew from Naples to Kissimmee, where something was going on with John Glenn's friend and hotel partner Henri Landwirth. It probably had something to do with one of his charities. Henri, a Holocaust survivor, had started Give Kids the World so the families of seriously ill children could grant their wish to visit Disney World or one of the other Orlando-area theme parks, no strings attached. When that event was over Joannie flew from Orlando on to Puerto Rico.

That was how it started. That December I went out to Sun Valley for some skiing and to meet her family. Marie and I had skied there in 1987. Pamela Harriman, the wonderful and famous Washington socialite who would be President Bill Clinton's ambassador to France, had loaned us her house and Ellen's husband Rene had gotten us Paul Matthes as a ski teacher. He was still teaching eight years later and I booked him for my visit. I was riding up the lift with him one day when Paul said, "All those Patterson children (there were five), one is nicer than the other." That did it for me.

All of them had a dominant sports gene. Joannie was an enthusiastic athlete and skier, as was her late husband Jim Patterson. In fact she had come to Sun Valley in the first place to be a professional skater in the Sun Valley Ice Show. Later, she and Jim built the house in which they raised those children and that later became the main lodge (since remodeled) at the base of Baldy on the Warm Springs side. Their oldest child was Ruff, who directed Dartmouth's ski program to the NCAA championship in 2007. Susie and her husband Ned Gillette, a noted explorer, trekked in far flung places. Barbie, the next in line, married Thor Kallerud, a U.S. ski team coach and a partner in a Wall Street firm in San Francisco. Pete had a fourth in the 1980 Olympics in the downhill and guided rafters and trekkers to exotic destinations. The youngest, Matt, was in the business side of sports with gear for backpackers and runners. Joannie had put most of them through college by selling real estate in Sun Valley after Jim got sick and had to give up his civil engineering business. Despite his athletic prowess, he was a heavy smoker and it killed him.

Paul's comment sealed the deal as far as I was concerned. Joannie and I started seeing each other as much as we could. The following November, 1996, she came to New York and stayed at the house in Irvington. Anticipating her visit, I had gone to Tiffany's on Fifth Avenue and picked out three rings. After she arrived, I told her I had to see a lawyer in the city and invited her to come along. Dennis drove us down and parked in a lot at the Carlton House where the firm used to keep an apartment back in the Bache & Co. days. The attendant still let us park there in exchange for a tip. The two of us took off for the lawyer's office, which I told her was at 55th Street and Fifth Avenue. To get there we had to pass Tiffany's at 57th Street. When we got there I grabbed her by the hand and said, "I've got to go in here."

I had arranged for a clerk to be waiting with the rings. Joannie's eyes got bigger and bigger as we approached the counter. I said, "You've got these three to choose from." I thought it was a good sign that she chose the one I liked the most.

We planned the wedding for April, 1997. She didn't want to be married in Sun Valley where she knew everybody but I had few ties. We could have gotten married in Lake Placid, where the situation was reversed, and I didn't want that. So we chose Irvington and the Ardsley Country Club. We had a small wedding with about forty people, all family. My good friend David Harkness, the minister at the Irvington Presbyterian Church who arrived three weeks after Marie's funeral, presided and it was great fun aside from the club manager forgetting to open the fireplace flues.

We embarked on an active sports life and looked forward to a lot of travel. The Australia Funds were among the mutual funds on whose boards I served. The directors' meeting was coming up in London and I booked an English manor house. It was going to be a kind of honeymoon.

Joannie and I were playing tennis just nine days after the wedding, working out with the local pro. Through a combination of new shoes, a soft court, and lunging too hard for a serve, I took a fall and heard a crack. Joannie laughed it off at first. "Come on, get up," she said. "There's nothing wrong with you."

So I tried to get up and fainted from the pain. I had broken my femur right in half, and spent nine days in the hospital.

That nixed the London trip for me, but Joannie went with Susie, stayed in the manor house, attended the directors' dinners, and had a fine time.

The fine times continued when I was back on my feet. Joannie was a superb wife. She was very strong-willed. She was always late and I was always early. We got used to each other. We'd go to Europe and Asia with the Australia Funds and we'd go all over the country to the mutual fund board meetings. We'd fly between Sun Valley and Lake Placid and Irvington. We bought a condo on Longboat Key near Sarasota, Florida, that I had rented when Marie was still alive, and we went there for winter getaways.

Joannie would never tell me how old she was. It wasn't that I really cared, but Marie had been two and a half years older. I assumed Joannie was younger, but I was curious about how much. When I asked she would just smile and shake her head as if to say, "A gentleman never asks a woman her age," and so after awhile I stopped asking.

When we had been married about five years Dr. Murray Silver, my doctor in New York, had examined Joannie and didn't like her blood chemistry. Her red blood count was very low, 7 or 8 as opposed to 14 or 15. She got worse during a trip to Florida. When we came back Dr. Silver sent her to a hematologist, who hospitalized her for an immediate transfusion. It solved the problem in the short term but her blood counts were always on the edge.

I largely retired in the spring of 2004. At least I stopped going to the city, and we stopped traipsing around to mutual fund board meetings in places like London, Paris, and Hong Kong. I opened a small office on Main Street in Irvington, and Saul Eisenberg and I continued to manage investments for a small and loyal group of clients.

In March of 2006 Joannie was diagnosed with lung cancer. I had a horrible sense of déjà vu. It was almost unbearable imagining that she faced the same disease that had killed Marie. When I went to put Dr. Kris, the chemotherapy expert for lung cancer, into my phone book, his name was already there. He had treated Marie. The first diagnosis was that it was only in her lungs. The doctors said it was inoperable, but my fears eased when she had a course of chemotherapy and the cancer went into remission.

That December, she went out to Sun Valley ahead of me and got a head start on the skiing. Like Marie, she was a better skier than I was. She skied twelve times. I joined her at the end, and we came back to Irvington after the first of the year. One beautiful day that January of 2007, softer than a winter day on the Hudson has a right to be, we were talking about going for a walk on the scenic Aqueduct Trail that follows the path of an old aqueduct that took drinking water from Croton to New York. As we were talking I noticed that her facial muscles were not working right. When we got home I called Robert Roven, our doctor who lives next door. He called Dr. Marvin Cooper, Joannie's primary doctor in Manhattan. We met him at Lenox Hill Hospital and then she was rushed to Sloan Kettering.

Tests there revealed that the cancer had metastasized to her brain. She received ten days of brain radiation treatments but during that time it got much worse in her lungs. She died at Sloan Kettering on February 20, 2007, surrounded by her children.

We talked a lot in the weeks of her illness. For one thing she relented and told me how old she was. She was four years younger than me, but I had thought she was a lot younger than that. I wondered what had caused the cancer. She said she never smoked. Her son Ruff said she smoked a little. But her husband Jim was a heavy, heavy smoker. I thought of all the warnings about second-hand smoke. Being around it for so long must have been what killed her.

I think about it all the time that Marie and Joannie both went the same way. It just doesn't seem fair. I return to the image of being wrapped up in a cocoon. I had a wonderful childhood, a great time at Lincoln School, and then I met Marie and the Air Force was great. The first few months after the war were poor but after that it was great all the way. Nothing could ever really touch me. Family would die, friends would die, markets would collapse, but I was always in that cocoon. And then Marie came home one day and said she had to have a CAT scan and I wasn't in a cocoon anymore. And it was the same with Joannie. At least Joannie didn't linger on through a long and sad decline. For that much I am grateful.

I courted Joannie for two years and we were married for ten, so I had the privilege of knowing her for twelve years altogether, and those years were grand. We played a lot of tennis. We skied. We had a great time with her family during Christmases at Sun Valley. She completely redid the Irvington house, which had run down after Marie's death. She spruced up the condominium in Florida. We walked on the aqueduct. We just had a wonderful time in the short time that we had. Every day was an adventure, until the adventure was over.

Joannie had not wanted a funeral. Her family and friends gathered at Sun Valley a few months after she died, and remembered her with soaring words of praise.

"The years flew by," I said when it came my turn to speak. I said one of the reasons we had been so happy was that we both had wonderful childhoods and great first marriages. I closed my remarks by quoting Jan Struther, the pen name of the author who wrote *Mrs. Miniver*. It was a quote I knew Joannie would have wanted read:

> One day my life will end; and lest
> Some whim should prompt you to review it,
> Let her who knows the subject best
> Tell you the shortest way to do it:
> Then say, "Here lies one doubly blest."
> Say, "She was happy." Say, "She knew it."

The Next Generations

Nancy, my eldest, has been a great joy as a daughter. During my marriage to Joannie she suffered a great tragedy when she lost her husband at the age of just fifty. His name was William H. Haneman, but was known to one and all as Woof. Woof was head of the trading department at Legg Mason, a medium-sized brokerage firm, when he dropped dead at his desk ten days before Christmas, 1997.

It was terrible to be widowed at such a young age. My heart goes out to her, but she picked herself up and has been making a good life for herself. She is surrounded by friends who love and support her, and she's active in community service and volunteer work. She worked for eight years as the development director for the Carver Center, a community center in Port Chester, New York, near her home in Rye, doing fundraising and outreach. We're very close, and she calls me every day

Nancy and Woof had two children. Patricia went to Trinity and after graduating spent a year as a ski instructor in Breckinridge, Colorado. There she met a real nice guy from

South Carolina named Brian Cox, called Chappy, who was working as a lift attendant. Chappy was into historic preservation, which he pursued in Savannah, Georgia, while Patricia returned to New York. Through Virg Sherrill, she got a job at Sloan Kettering as a child life specialist. It was a tough job, counseling children with cancer and their families, because half of those young people would die, but she kept at it for nine years while getting a Master's in special education at Bank Street College. Meanwhile, Chappy moved to New York to work on a Master's in historic preservation at Columbia, and they got married and moved to Newfields, New Hampshire. He restores old pieces of New England history, barns, steeples, and the like. Patricia got another Master's, this one in social work. She is a special education case manager for the Portsmouth school district and is on the board of the Child Life Council. Meanwhile, she and Chappy had a son, Breck, who as I write this is four years old. They're very happy and a joy to me; Patricia, like her mother, calls me every day and she is just a very good and very caring person.

Her sister is named Nicolle. She went to Dartmouth and then worked for Wall Street firms for three or four years when she met her husband, Alex Keally. They moved to Boston and she went back to the Tuck School, Dartmouth's business school. But she didn't go back to Wall Street, thank goodness. Instead she went to work for a bio-tech company, Vertex Pharmaceuticals, where she is the director of finance, while Alex heads sales and marketing for Evergreen Solar. They had a baby girl, Hadley, in 2008 and I'm proud to say they're happy, too.

My son Terry met his wife Sally in 1974 when he was in architecture school at Penn and she was an undergraduate. When she got her degree she went on to M.I.T. to architecture school. They married in 1982, and it was a match made in heaven, or maybe on a drawing board. Terry had founded his firm with partner Jamie Wyper a year earlier. Today Jacobs/ Wyper is doing great, with a total staff of twenty-five and a range of residential, corporate and educational clients

Terry and Sally have two fine boys. Andrew spent twenty-seven months as a Peace Corps volunteer in Togo, West Africa, helping villagers learn more productive farming techniques. He came home in December 2009. Earlier, he wrote me about the importance of service and how much he missed skiing. "Two years without skiing is practically a sin in our family," he said. At the time his brother Steven, who was a mediocre student at the Germantown Friends School in Philadelphia, was starting his senior year at Skidmore College in Saratoga Springs, New York, and getting straight A's.

Terry and Sally have a very happy life and a very good marriage, so I've been very blessed by all my children. And I've been doubly blessed by the next generation with a particularly snappy nickname. All my grandchildren call me Pop Pop. (They called Marie Ga Ga – it was not a reflection on her state of mind.) In fact, my four-year-old great grandson, Patricia and Chappy's son Breck, has embellished that to Pop Pop the Great. How much better can it get for a great granddad?

Terry was two years behind Ned Gillette, Joannie's daughter Susie's husband, at both the Holderness School and Dartmouth. Susie and Ned both loved the outdoors and exploring the farthest reaches of the world. In August 1999, they were exploring northern Pakistan. They were near the tribal areas of the Swat Valley, camping on a mountain at an elevation of 16,000 feet, when bandits attacked and shot them as they slept. Ned died, and Susie was wounded. She lay there holding her dead husband for three or four days before some villagers found her. They took her to a tiny town called Gilgit way north of Islamabad.

Joannie and I were in Sun Valley when we finally got word. We had a terrible time getting her out and home again. John Glenn had left the Senate after his fourth term at the beginning of the year, but he was still a great help in bringing her home.

I remain close with both Susie and her sister Barbie. When I asked them to supply a few notes for this memoir, Barbie responded eloquently. She recounted her mother's embrace of all life had to offer and flattered me by describing me in the same terms. "No wonder they fell in love," she wrote. "They both had led amazing and successful lives, had incredible families, had lost their lovely spouses too soon, and more importantly they both had a zest for life!"

Lessons

At this stage of my life I've managed to outlive most of my contemporaries. I am officially an old guy. That's a great place to be, because I can offer some life lessons without too much fear of contradiction.

When Marie and I lived in Ardsley, I used to go down to the drugstore every Saturday and have a pastrami sandwich and read the financials. I always sat next to Charlie Hoy, who owned the plumbing shop in town. We would talk and one day he asked me, "Do you like your job?"

"Yes," I said. "I love my job. What about you?"

He got this look, like a guy out of an old movie who's running to get through a closing door and he knows he's not going to make it. "I hate it," he said.

That's my first lesson. There are too many people who go through life hating their jobs. Not everybody has the good luck to be able to choose what they do, but life's too short not to try. If you love what you do, you never work a day in your life.

And if you love your job, you always have something to look forward to. That's important, too. But it doesn't have to be your job, just as long as you have something to look forward to. John Glenn says about me that I always know what I'm going to be doing, or think I know what I'm going to be doing, a year ahead. I always like to plan what I'm going to be doing in the future. Anticipation is one of the best things there is.

This sounds obvious, but develop good judgment and uncommon common sense. Common sense is in all-to-short short supply. That's why I say "uncommon common sense." Just use your head. This is going to overlap with some other things I want to say about the latest financial crisis in 2008 and 2009 that brought comparisons with the Great Depression of the 1930s, which I lived through. But look at the financial catastrophes in the recent crisis and try to figure out who used uncommon common sense. Not many people. Bear Stearns went under because people were greedy beyond anything you can imagine. When I started a CEO could expect to make forty times what a worker did. That's reasonable, but CEOs and executives more recently were taking out sums that had no relation at all to that equation. To take that money, they took risks that didn't make sense. Common sense means taking risks that make sense, not risks that are obscene.

Maybe this is a contradiction, but you also have to be competitive. Obviously we live in a competitive world, so you have to compete like hell when you're going up the ladder.

What happens when competition — for the short-term gains the market loves or the fees you get from packaging and peddling high-risk securities or financial voodoo like credit default swaps — forces you to look common sense in the eye and turn away? That's a tough one. Try to hang on to your integrity. Dissent if you have to. Wall Street doesn't love lone wolves, but individual pride and the knowledge that you protected your customers will lead to better sleep at night.

There were a number of votes on the New York Stock Exchange Board where I was the lone dissenter. And I was right on every one. When the trouble started in the late 1960s, the

NYSE set up a trust fund to make the customers from the failed firms whole. Then the trust fund started running out of money, so the governors got scared – this was before SIPC (Securities Investor Protection Corporation) – and refused to put any more money in the trust fund. And I was up there screaming, "You can't do that." Because if the customers were left holding the bag like bank depositors back in the Depression, you'd start a super-panic. But they voted to leave the customers high and dry. Then a couple of firms did go broke, and the customers were picketing the stock exchange. After that the SIPC legislation passed, but that was about the dumbest thing I ever saw.

There was a rule that an investor could only invest in one firm at a time. Ross Perot, who I called "a chill wind from the Southwest," took over Francis I. DuPont, which was failing. And then he wanted to merge with Walston, and the stock exchange wanted to pass a rule that Walston could merge with DuPont. But Perot had an investment in DuPont and an investment in Walston, which they had allowed. And I said, "You can't do that. It's against regulations." But they did it anyhow. So DuPont merged with Walston and the whole thing came crashing down. It was a huge bankruptcy.

I was very much a maverick, but under the conditions that existed at the time you could be independent and even find some allies.

Above all, have courage. The most important thing I learned being CEO of a large financial concern is that you have to face up to developing bad situations early on. Pretend you are a bull and charge at the fence until you knock it down. I have seen several very senior executives ruin their careers because they wouldn't do this. Indeed, failure to acknowledge and confront a looming crisis ruined not only individual careers but entire firms. Imagine if, during the 2008 meltdown, senior people at Bear Stearns and Lehman Brothers had faced up early to the bad assets on their books and kicked them out. They would still be here and so would a lot of other Wall Street firms including Merrill Lynch.

I often wondered as I rose in my career if I had courage. You always wonder until you prove it to yourself. It had taken some courage to buck Harold Bache and the rest of the firm's executives when I decided to start taking five weeks of vacation with my family. But that was different. I was dealing with friends in that case, not enemies. They didn't like it, but they understood, and I kept up my end of the bargain by working extra hard the rest of the time

And then came along the Belzberg affair. I knew I would rather die than be in the same boardroom with Sam Belzberg. So in my own way I fought him every inch of the way with everything at my command. That was my defining moment. It taught me I had the courage to get through anything.

I can't fully express the value of that lesson. As anyone knows who goes through the death of a loved one, courage is one of the components that gets you through it. I needed courage to cope with Marie's illness and death, and later Joannie's. It helped a lot to know I had it and could find it in a crisis.

Of course, you can have courage and be dead wrong. That happened to me, too. When DuPont Walston was collapsing or had collapsed under Ross Perot in 1974, there was a big meeting at the stock exchange. Wally Auch, who had taken over the firm in its death throes, was supervising the liquidation and they were putting up their offices on a chalkboard and all the firms were taking different pieces. We were well positioned to grab off a huge hunk of offices, which we needed to extend our sales reach. I asked the stock exchange execs if DuPont Walston was in sound financial condition, and they said yes. But in the meantime I had Bache's corporate finance guys checking all over and we had proof that Walston had defaulted on some of its payments on their bonds and subordinated debt. That meant that they were busted. And if we took over a firm like that, say we took over the Milwaukee office and we sent out a statement to all the DuPont customers that they were now Bache statements and those securities never got to us, we could have bankrupted the firm and been ruined.

John Leslie, whom I respected very much, and Ed O'Brien, who was chair of the executive committee, both wanted to do it. Most of the people in the firm, the branch guys, wanted to do it. And I said no. I thought we were exposing the firm to terrific risk. And I said to myself, if these guys do that, I'm walking out. But I should have realized that on something that big the regulators were going to make sure their transactions went through. So the spoils of DuPont Walston were divided among Wall Street, but we took none of them.

E. F. Hutton, where Bob Foman was in charge, took a huge bunch. That guy was a riverboat gambler, but in this case he gambled correctly. The securities were all delivered in spite of the bankruptcy. And with the new offices, Hutton passed Bache in size. It became one of the country's largest retail brokerages, only to be destroyed by the mail and wire fraud scandal that occurred a few years later.

We could have used those offices. It took courage to buck opinion within the firm, but it was a totally wrong decision that resulted in a setback to the firm, and it was totally my fault.

So my last lesson is admit your mistakes, pick yourself up, and move on.

Changes on Wall Street

John Glenn thought I should devote part of this story to the changes I have seen in Wall Street. It's not part of my life's story, but I have definite opinions about the causes of the 2008-09 financial crisis that some now call the Great Recession.

The main cause is a lack of memory. Some years ago Sandy Weil, the CEO of Smith Barney, wanted to merge with Citicorp, the parent company of Citibank. The merger was blocked by the Glass-Steagall Act. Glass-Steagall was passed in 1933. It split commercial banks from investment banks because their comingling had caused a lot of trouble and ruined a lot of lives in the 1929 crash and the Great Depression that followed. It was a good law.

Of course the banks didn't like it. They started pushing for repeal in the 1980s. Texas Senator Phil Gramm, a Republican, led the charge for repeal in the Congress and by 1999 he had the wind at his back. Hearings were held. Senator Paul Sarbanes was the ranking Democrat on the Banking Committee and my friend Steve Harris was his chief of staff. They asked me to come down and talk and I went to Washington to tell them not to change the law. But the law was changed that year and President Clinton signed it. It proved to be a bad idea.

It was a bad idea because the creation of these one-stop financial shopping centers coincided with the rise of a culture of debt. This replaced the culture of thrift that had been in place since the Great Depression. The culture of debt was kicked off by the credit card companies. They told people to "Buy Now, Pay Later." Which was fine until people couldn't pay off their credit card bills at the end of the month and started carrying balances that got higher and higher and made the card companies rich and their users poorer.

Then the culture of debt went on steroids, aka the "housing bubble." Millions of people were buying houses that they couldn't afford. They were encouraged by a large group of irresponsible lenders, banks and mortgage companies that were loaning people money on all kinds of crazy terms. Who ever heard of a "no-document" housing loan, or a housing loan without proof of income? People bought houses thinking prices were always going to go up, and the lenders thought the same thing. In a matter of months we and much of the developed world went from housing bubble to mortgage crisis. Prices were only beginning to stabilize toward the end of 2009 as I am writing this, but the housing sector will be overbuilt for a long time.

The third component was the worst of all. We have in place regulatory authorities, a whole bunch of them, and they should have worked together. But they were either asleep at the switch or too territorial.

The cause of the mortgage crisis was the greed of the lenders and the borrowers. But it was the negligence of government agencies that enabled lenders and borrowers to bring havoc to the financial markets. That negligence was encouraged by administrations starting with Ronald Reagan and peaking with George W. Bush that were anti-regulation. Now we know better. But the regulatory system we have needs a total overhaul.

The kind of one-stop financial shopping espoused by Sandy Weil and Citicorp and championed by Phil Gramm never worked out. Why should Citicorp be allowed to own a bank, an insurance company, a brokerage house, and on and on? Eleven years later, after a huge injection of government money, Citicorp is still a basket case.

While too much easy credit brought on the mortgage crisis, it also played a role in the financial industry's implosion. When consumers borrow money, it's called debt. When hedge funds, private equity firms, and investment bankers borrow money, it's called leverage, which is just another word for taking risks with other people's money.

The risk obviously increases with the proportion of borrowed money to a firm's capital base. Recently, that proportion got seriously out of whack. Bache used to operate on a capital ratio of ten or twelve to one, meaning that if we borrowed $100 or $120 million we had $10 million in the bank to cushion any downturn. A lot of that ratio – margin accounts, for example – were pretty low risk.

From what I've read about the demise of Bear Stearns, their leverage – their risk – was thirty- or forty-to-one and their inventory risk was to a large extent in low quality securities like toxic mortgages that in the crisis became unmarketable.

Their executives were seasoned and well trained and they had worked together for many years. How could they have done this? How could they have funded themselves with so much short-term money? Where was their board of directors? Where were the regulators, particularly the SEC? It's a terrible story that could have been avoided.

Hedge funds, even though they've been around for years, are synonymous with the new world of finance. Unlike commercial banks and stock brokerages, they're lightly regulated. They're called hedge funds because they're supposed to find non-traditional investments like real estate that hedge, or spread, the risk associated with traditional stocks. I am too far away from the day-to-day business at this point to be knowledgeable. But I do know that hedge funds generally charge a 2 percent annual fee plus 20 percent of any profits.

Hedge fund managers defend taking 20 percent of profits by claiming that it provides incentive. However, I've never heard of a hedge fund that offered a rebate amounting to 20 percent of losses in a down year. I think 20 percent is too much, and Warren Buffet of Berkshire-Hathaway and Jack Bogle of the Vanguard Group can tell you that over time the investor will not do well as the fees accumulate against them year after year.

Also, some of the things hedge funds do to achieve profits are harmful to the markets as a whole. For example, did naked short selling by hedge funds aggravate the 2008 financial crisis? I would guess so.

I believe full disclosure of hedge fund activity should be required by legislation.

I have said I think greed played a part in the recent crisis. I mentioned earlier reading an article that said a CEO should expect pay around 40 times the salary of a worker. If a company's workers average $50,000, the CEO therefore should take home $2 million. That's not an unreasonable differential. CEOs have responsibilities workers don't have.

But by the early 2000s, CEOs and other top executives were raking in compensation in the tens and hundreds of millions of dollars. They negotiated golden parachutes that rained more tens of millions on them if they left for whatever reason, even scandal and failure to perform. Whether their firms prospered or suffered, they got paid regardless.

How could top Wall Street executives have the audacity to take so much money out of their firms? It was and is unsound. It's illogical. It's shameless. It's obscene. Again, where oh where were the boards of these firms? To this day I don't understand how this could have happened and how people could be such pigs.

So we have come full circle rather fast.

A thumbnail history might read like this: Investment firms didn't respect their customers. New types of investment vehicles within the financial system grew in a violent and uncontrolled manner. Valuable and important legislation was disregarded or discarded.

One-stop financial shopping made no sense.

Greed and excessive risk enveloped the landscape.

Boards of directors abdicated their duties. Regulators went AWOL and a violent and disruptive wind blew across the financial landscape. I have said for many years that a large corporation left unregulated and unsupervised will become like an octopus strangling and eating everything in its path. I think the events leading up to the 2008 – 2009 crisis prove the truth of that, and I hope we can reestablish oversight and regulation of big corporations in general and financial corporations in particular.

I must commend the Bush administration for one thing: appointing in Ben Bernanke a Federal Reserve Board Chairman who had written his thesis on the Great Depression.

I commend the Obama administration for acting with alacrity and strength to prevent a market meltdown.

At this point – the late fall of 2009 – we seem to have learned from the days of FDR and things are getting better. But down the road, we must worry about the growing deficit and address and solve that problem.

My Investment Philosophy

My approach to investments is simple. I gave many talks on it over my career. It's this: good securities carefully selected and held for long periods of time will usually turn out to be the best investment a person can make over his or her lifetime. This is true in terms of both capital appreciation and dividend income. I don't look at my portfolio every day, every week, or even every month. I only look at it every three months or so, but I avidly look at the papers every week for percentage of dividend increases. That's A and B of my discussion.

The past year – it's now November, 2009 -- has sorely tested that thesis, because I own a lot of bank stocks, probably too many, and their dividend performance has lagged. Let's take State Street Corporation as an example. It's not really a bank, but a financial services holding company. They had increased their dividend by small amounts twice a year, every year since 1978. All of a sudden they got in trouble, stupidly, because they had bought toxic assets for their portfolio and they were forced to take that dividend and slash it down to nothing. And that has happened with almost every major bank that I can think of. Bank of America got in trouble. They cut their dividend. Citicorp sold below a dollar. Good banks like J. P. Morgan slashed their dividends, too. Good regional banks like SunTrust got in serious trouble. So we saw dividend cuts on a scale that we could never have imagined.

And even other companies like Pfizer, a major factor in the pharmaceutical business, cut their dividends in half.

So the second half of my thesis was castrated, at least temporarily. As for the first part, all these television gurus are saying the days of buy and hold are over. You cannot buy a stock and hold it for a long period of time, you've got to buy it and if it goes up, flip it and go on to something else. That goes against common sense because with our tax structure you'd be paying taxes on a lot of short-term gains or long-term gains.

While my thesis was severely shaken, I think I still believe in buy and hold. As for looking for dividend increases, that's in a state of negative abeyance.

Buying a stock and selling options, I think all that stuff is frivolous.

Even buy and hold is not true in every case. You have to have some discernment, and not buy in industries that are on the way down, like autos and steel after World War II. Use your head and have a good advisor. We're all vulnerable. As I said, I have too much money in bank stocks, and this economic and financial catastrophe caught me unaware and I hadn't diversified enough. So we're all human.

For example, I got bagged in AIG (American International Group). Saul Eisenberg bought me some of that in 1981 with the Prudential buyout money. When the first whiff of problems occurred when Eliot Spitzer was still New York attorney general investigating possible accounting fraud, I sold half of it. I put in $30,000 and the $30,000 accumulated into something under $1 million, and I took out about $350,000. But I got bagged on the other half. I got so mad at myself for getting socked on the last $350,000. I did okay, but not as well as I should have.

I try to cut my losses and move on, but I'm very self-critical for not having recognized the tremendous leverage that financial institutions used to go about their daily business. Like Bear Stearns, Lehman, AIG, all those. I think you could have picked it out by looking at their balance sheets, but I didn't.

The best way to stay on top of what's happening in the financial world is the daily newspapers, including the financial ones. I don't really use the Internet, but I think the volume of information you get there is just overwhelming. And spend the time to read your companies' annual reports. You gain a lot of knowledge just by leafing through them.

And that last part of my philosophy is to have a good investment advisor. That's easier said than done, because they're extremely hard to find, as the Bernie Madoff saga demonstrated.

Remarkable Women

The immense respect I bore for Marie and her strength as a wife, a mother, an athlete, and an all-around human being caused me to always feel women should be on a par with men in the securities business and in other endeavors. I encountered a number of remarkable women over my career and would like to mention some of them here.

Delayne Gold was invaluable to me as the head of public relations for Bache and Company and Prudential Securities after that. Later she was in charge of mutual funds and she sat on the Operating Committee board as well as on the mutual fund boards.

I learned much of what I know about strategic planning from Robin Smith, the former CEO of Publishers Clearing House. She was an outside director of many top corporate boards. I found her very supportive and a strong, strong person.

Jessica Bibliowitz is Sandy Weil's daughter and a star in her own right – hard-working, smart, creative, and a good and loyal friend. She was the sales manager of the Mutual Fund Company at Pru-Bache when I came back as interim chairman.

Sharon Pratt Kelly was the mayor of Washington, D.C. from 1991 to 1995. She was the first woman of any race and the first African-American woman to serve as mayor of the nation's capital. Before that, I helped and worked with her when she was secretary of the Democratic National Committee when I chaired the Democratic Business Council. She was a lovely person and a joy to work with.

Wilma Greenfield was the DBC's executive director during my chairmanship. She was a real professional, always upbeat, and I miss her friendship.

Many people saw Pamela Harriman as something of a dragon lady. She was *tres formidable*, all right, but that allowed her to accomplish a great deal. She was the driving force behind the revival of the Democratic Party from the crisis of its 1980 and 1984 defeats. She was a remarkable woman who did much for the party and for America.

Janet Howard was Mrs. Harriman's longtime aide de camp, and she made everything happen. She went from Mrs. Harriman to become an executive at the Coca Cola Company.

And there was JoAnne de Stefano, my administrative assistant and secretary for seventeen years when I was at Bache and Pru-Bache. I couldn't have moved without her. She was smart and loyal, worked hard, and did everything flawlessly. She was also instrumental in helping me get through Marie's death. She was an assistant vice president of the Investment Advisory Group when she retired.

The glass ceiling isn't what it used to be for women, and I hope that in the future more smart and talented women will be able to rise to the top in all fields. It's high time there was a level playing field, particularly in the financial world where men have dominated.

Friends and Meaningful Others

I've been blessed to have not only a wonderful and loving family, but over the years a matchless collection of friends and people who by example, personality, or character have made a big impact on my life. I've mentioned some of them already, like Ramon Guthrie, my Proust professor back at Dartmouth, Virg Sherrill (who died as I was putting the finishing touches on this book) and Annie and John Glenn. I'd be remiss if I didn't add a few names, hastening to add at the same time that it's just a very few. If I tried to be comprehensive I'm sure I'd leave somebody out and I don't want to do that. The ones who are dead won't care, but I want to be fair to everybody, so it's a short list, presented in no particular order.

B. George Lapan was president of the Adirondack National Bank and Trust in Saranac Lake. He was my second customer. He was also the perfect small town banker. If somebody came in and needed a loan badly and the bank couldn't do it legitimately according to the formula, George most of the time would give the guy the money anyway. He was just a wonderful man. Every time I would go to see him he would open up the bank's books and explain how things worked. He taught me a lot and I loved him dearly. He died in a tragic Jeep accident while he was hunting, but the citizens of Saranac Lake recognized his contributions; the road out of town is still called the George Lapan Highway.

I have mentioned Clark Clifford. He provided me wise and able counsel on many occasions after we met when Bache needed a representative in Washington. He also gave me the convincing rationale for my longtime allegiance to the Democratic Party. Beyond that, his fingerprints are on some of the landmark events and programs of the Twentieth Century, including Truman's decision to recognize Israel. Later, as President Kennedy's private counsel, he came up with the idea for the Peace Corps, such an enduring idea that, as I wrote earlier, my grandson Andrew was among its volunteers. And it was Clark, as Lyndon Johnson's secretary of defense, who convinced LBJ that the country was so divided over the war in Vietnam that he could not run again.

This all was stellar and selfless service to the country. Later, however, Clark stumbled. In a tangle of connections that went back to the late 1970s, he represented some Middle Easterners who took over a bank in Washington, D.C. called First American Bankshares. He also chaired the board. It turned out the buyers were fronting for a rogue bank called the Bank of Credit and Commerce International (BCCI), which dodged regulation and had a history of shady practices. BCCI was later shut down for illegally controlling first American, and Clark was indicted in New York on both state and federal fraud charges. He had to come to the city to be fingerprinted, a humiliating moment. By then he was old and in deteriorating health and so wasn't prosecuted. He was still on the downhill from that scandal when Pamela Harriman, with whom he had been close, sued him over his handling of a trust for Averell Harriman's grandchildren. That cost him about $5 million.

Clark died a sick and broken man in 1998. I had kept in close touch with him in the face of his troubles, indeed because of them, and introduced Joannie to him after we were married, but what happened taught me a lesson. The BCCI people were able to dupe him because he wanted to hang on to the power and prestige he had enjoyed under five Democratic presidents. I realized you can never do that and determined never to try. Clark's ending was a sad story. But I still think he was a great American, and he was certainly a friend to me.

Keith Funston was one of my great business idols. He came from Nebraska. He looked like a president of the United States and he met Sidney Weinberg, a legendary senior partner at Goldman Sachs, when he was working on the War Production Board in World War II. After the war he became president of Trinity College in Hartford when he was still very young. Then the New York Stock Exchange was looking for a CEO, and so Sidney Weinberg created that job for Keith who didn't have a background in finance but was a very imposing leader type of person. As chairman of the NYSE, he had one goal, and that was to expand the American stockholder population and so for five or ten years he traveled the circuit of mashed potatoes and chicken all over the United States preaching, "Own your share of America." And I always had the greatest admiration for him.

Years later, I called him up and said, "My granddaughter is applying to Trinity College. Could you help?" He asked if she was applying for early admission. I didn't think so. He said, "If she's applying the regular way I'll write a letter and that will mean a great deal. But if she decides to apply for early admission she'll be admitted on the telephone." She applied the regular way and was admitted and I called him up to say how pleased I was and he said, "Well, I knew that a month ago." So I always stayed in touch with him. He could have been a Republican candidate for president.

I mentioned Ed O'Brien earlier, in my *mea culpa* about my refusal to take over any of the DuPont Walston offices when that firm went bankrupt in the 1970s. Ed was tough and persistent in arguing against my point of view, and that was one of the reasons I most admired him – and still do; he was and is a man of great personal courage. Later he took over as CEO of the Securities Industry Association, where he served for years with distinction and did a lot for the well-being of the industry. He and Margaret and Edward Jr. remain close personal friends.

John Glenn is not only a close friend, but through him and Annie I have met others whose friendships I treasure. Scott Carpenter was the second American to orbit the earth, after John, and being a Navy man, became a deep sea explorer after he left the space program. He and Patty are good friends and I fly over from Longboat Key to Palm Beach twice a winter to have lunch with them. Scott was one of the speakers when President Bush rededicated the World War II aircraft carrier *Intrepid* on Veterans Day, 2008, when it reopened to the public after two years of repairs. He invited me down to New York for the event, which was moving and exciting.

I also met former Congressman Tony Hall through John in 1994. Tony and his wife Janet had a son, Matt, who was at Sloan Kettering with leukemia. He was a great kid who died two years later, in July 1996. Tony represented the Ohio district that included Dayton. His issue was world hunger, and in 2002, after twenty-four years in the House of Representatives, President Bush named him Ambassador to the United Nations Food Program in Rome. He served for four years in that capacity and continues to campaign for ending hunger. His book, *Changing the Face of Hunger*, is another step in that direction. He and Janet are wonderful friends.

Bill Lowenthal was my lifelong friend. We were both infants when our nurses took us down to Central Park to play together. We went to Lincoln School for eight years and Dartmouth for four and we learned to fly together. For many years I didn't see him much because he was in the State Department, posted as an economic attaché in Argentina and Chile. When he and Alice returned I handled their financial affairs and was trustee of their children's trusts. When I started going to Longboat

Key, first with Marie and later Joannie, he and Alice had the condo under me. In April 2008, I went to Washington where they had a party for 100 people at the Cosmos Club to celebrate their sixtieth anniversary. Three weeks later I was back in Washington, giving the eulogy at his funeral. He was my oldest friend, and we were inseparable. Of course I still see Alice, who is a tower of strength and courage.

A few weeks after that I gave a eulogy for John Liebmann, who spent eight years with me at Lincoln School and many years at Lake Placid. I still see his widow, Ellin, when I'm at the lake.

Mo Distin was a skiing star in four events at Dartmouth, the best I ever saw. He and Mili lived in Saranac Lake. He got me on the board of the Trudeau Institute that I mentioned earlier when I was writing about my extracurricular activities in the section titled Outside Interests.

Wally Latour had left Merrill Lynch to run Francis I. DuPont, the brokerage firm that was ruined when Ross Perot took over. I'm sure all that stress killed him early.

I met Dan Cowin the week I started on Wall Street, and he met Warren Buffett early on. They took a class together. It was Danny's idea to buy Berkshire Hathaway for Mr. Buffett to use as his investment vehicle.

Bill Todd was merged out when Kuhn Loeb was sold to Lehman Brothers and I was able to help him in his new environment.

Bill Rose lived on Moose Island when we grew up in Lake Placid, and I knew him since we were five. We had dinner with him up there two years ago and a month later he was gone.

Bill Scheefer is still around as I write this, and that makes me happy. We go back to the 1940 Middlebury Carnival, when he skied for St. Lawrence and I was managing the Dartmouth ski team, but it turned out we had the Lake Placid area in common, too. He ran Scheefer's Jewelry Store in Saranac Lake until a few years ago when he turned eighty. We talk four or five days a week, mostly about the stock market.

Peter Roland has been my friend since we were teenagers. He owned the Lake Placid Hilton and some years ago we bought the peninsula at the southwest corner of Lake Placid and partially developed it.

I met Dr. Sam Gordon in 1940. He was an ear, nose and throat doctor during his career. Sam is ninety-one now and still drives to his place in Vermont when he is not in Palm Beach.

Speaking of doctors, I've been treated by some of the best. Murray Silver was my internist for forty-five years, and after he died I turned to Robert Roven, my next-door neighbor in Irvington. I've gone to Dr. Roven for ten years now. When I'm at Lake Placid I go to Dr. Tony Waickman at Saranac Lake. He's a small town doctor but he's the very best. Dr. Howard Scher at Sloan-Kettering is my oncologist. He may be the leading authority on prostate cancer in America and he probably saved my life when he took me off Flutamide. After I was originally diagnosed with prostate cancer almost twenty years ago, the big horse pills were making my PSA (prostate specific antigen) go up instead of down. Today I still take injections of Lupron to regulate hormone production and prevent a recurrence.

Saul Eisenberg deserves a special nod. He's been much more than a business colleague over the years, he's also been a warm and intellectually stimulating friend. Even though I don't really manage much money anymore, we still talk on the phone almost every day, mostly about investments and our views of what's going on in the financial world.

I would be remiss if I didn't mention the people who have made my life easier and more enjoyable in my later years. One is Mabel Drake in Irvington. We only had day help when Marie was alive because her farm girl's background hadn't accustomed her to live-in help. But after Marie died Mable expanded her duties. She comes Mondays, Tuesdays, Thursdays and Fridays. She's been with me for over fifty years.

Shirley Brewster comes Wednesdays, Saturdays and Sundays, and stays overnight Saturday night. She has been on the job for a good thirty-five years. Without Shirley and Mabel, life would be tough for me.

In Lake Placid I have Vi Geesler. I call her a short-timer since she's been with me for almost twenty years. Her family plows snow, solves electrical and other problems with the house, and she acts as my housekeeper and babysitter with the good humor she shares with the whole Geesler clan.

Sherry Wiley takes care of me when I'm at Longboat Key in Florida. She shared that job with her late husband Ken, who died two years ago. We were friends and I miss him, but I'm lucky to still have Sherry. Kathleen Brady was my sister's long-time nurse and also helped Joannie. She also helps me from time to time.

So I'm blessed with all kinds of wonderful retainers who are good friends and who help make my life better.

I also want to acknowledge (with pleasure) my assistant of seventeen years and close friend Sandy Wakefield. Sandy reverse commutes from Manhattan to our wonderful little office in Irvington, and it has been a great joy for me to work with her all these years. She is extremely competent, hard working, and is always upbeat. Sandy, like JoAnne, worked at the Investment Supervisory Group, although by then Wachovia had taken it over from Prudential, and she, too, retired as an assistant VP. It was Sandy's prodding that was the catalyst for me to stop procrastinating after Joannie died and get started on this book. "Get back on your horse," she said. "Life is for the living." That snapped me out of my blue funk and got me going.

Some Thoughts at the End of the Day

It's hard to tie a memoir up in a neat bow. I think about a lot of things. Mostly I think, over and over, about how lucky I am and have been.

First, of course, I'm lucky to have found two wonderful women, Marie and Joannie, to share big portions of my life. My marriages, first to Marie and then to Joannie, are easily the most important things in my life. A happy marriage transcends every other experience. I bathe in the memory of their love and my love for them. And I'm lucky in my children and stepchildren, my grandchildren and great grandchildren.

On a level of pure enjoyment, I'm lucky to still be able to fly. I fly out of Lake Placid with Steve Short of the Adirondack Flying Service in a Cessna 414. (We had a close call in 2008 when we lost cabin pressure at 18,000 feet flying to Lake Placid from Sarasota and my vision blurred and the pain in my heart made me think I was having a heart attack. But we dropped down and I recovered. That was my third close call in an airplane and I don't want another one.) In Florida I fly with Luis Savigne, an airplane manager, in a Cessna 421. I try to get 100 hours a year but I never quite make it; still, I have clocked almost 5,000 hours as a pilot and I'm proud of that. I'm not too proud to turn over the controls or get in the right seat when the weather gets rough. And when I'm not in the air I stay up-to-date by reading *IFR Refresher* every month, and I read *Flying* magazine to fulfill my fantasies.

I'm lucky to experience a parade of family at beautiful Lake Placid and the family camp at Buck Island. My sister Kitty's children, the twins Tom and Peter, and their brother John, and their families, and my brother Bob's daughter Barbara Tamerin and her boyfriend Hans Laverge, and occasionally Bobby Jacobs Jr. and his family all visit the camp. Friends abound as well. I picture a big smile on my mother's face if she could see the way her house is used after all these years, and the happiness its walls have seen.

I'm lucky to still be mobile and active. I am not and never was an outstanding athlete like Marie and Joannie were, but I stretch a great deal and it keeps me reasonably limber. I do it every day in Florida and Lake Placid and twice a week in Irvington. It takes almost an hour and it's my personal version of yoga. I also walk a lot and play tennis, not so much foursomes anymore but I work out with a pro. I also swim a lot in Florida, and at Lake Placid and Irvington, weather permitting.

I also might drink five glasses of wine a week (but never more than one a day). The French must know something.

I am lucky to have found the gift of prayer. It makes me feel good to be able to talk to God. I pray for our promising young President, Barack Obama, who has been so much vilified of late by crazy, hateful people on the right. I pray every day for his safety. I pray for all the people in my family, each one of my children and grandchildren, my friends and the people I love. I pray that He'll take care of me. I hope I can leave this earth easily. Most people don't.

I am lucky to have a wonderful pastor in the Reverend David Harkness at the Irvington Presbyterian Church. He has made a tremendous impression on my life. When I think about what I want to happen when I die, I form a picture: David takes me by the arm and leads me across a river to the other side. He leaves me there and I watch him go back across the river and then I turn around and take in my new surroundings. I don't know what they'll look like. I hope he can do that. Maybe my faith will make it happen.

If I can look down at my funeral, I'd like to see people brushing away tears and I'd like to hear eloquent eulogies. I want people to be sad that I'm gone. But I don't want them to forget that I had a truly wonderful, blessed life. I don't want them to forget the joy and the laughter I experienced. I want to hear funny stories along with the somber tones of loss. I want to hear and see a celebration. I hope it will be just the kind of celebration that I'm feeling now as I put this book to bed.

But with any sort of luck this book will stand in for that final celebration for a few years still to come.

-- Harry A. Jacobs Jr.
   November 2009

CPSIA information can be obtained at www.ICGtesting.com
262112BV00001B/23/P

9 781432 752064